Homer De Lois Sweet

Twilight Hours in the Adirondacks

Homer De Lois Sweet

Twilight Hours in the Adirondacks

ISBN/EAN: 9783337191276

Printed in Europe, USA, Canada, Australia, Japan

Cover: Foto ©Andreas Hilbeck / pixelio.de

More available books at **www.hansebooks.com**

TWILIGHT HOURS
IN THE
ADIRONDACKS.

THE
DAILY
DOINGS
AND SEVERAL SAYINGS OF
SEVEN SOBER, SOCIAL, SCIENTIFIC STUDENTS
IN THE
GREAT WILDERNESS
OF
NORTHERN NEW YORK,
VARIOUSLY VERSIFIED IN
SEVEN THOUSAND
SEVEN HUNDRED
AND SEVENTY
SEVEN
LINES
BY
HOMER D. L. SWEET.
Farmer and Chronicler.

SYRACUSE:
WYNKOOPS & LEONARD.
1870.

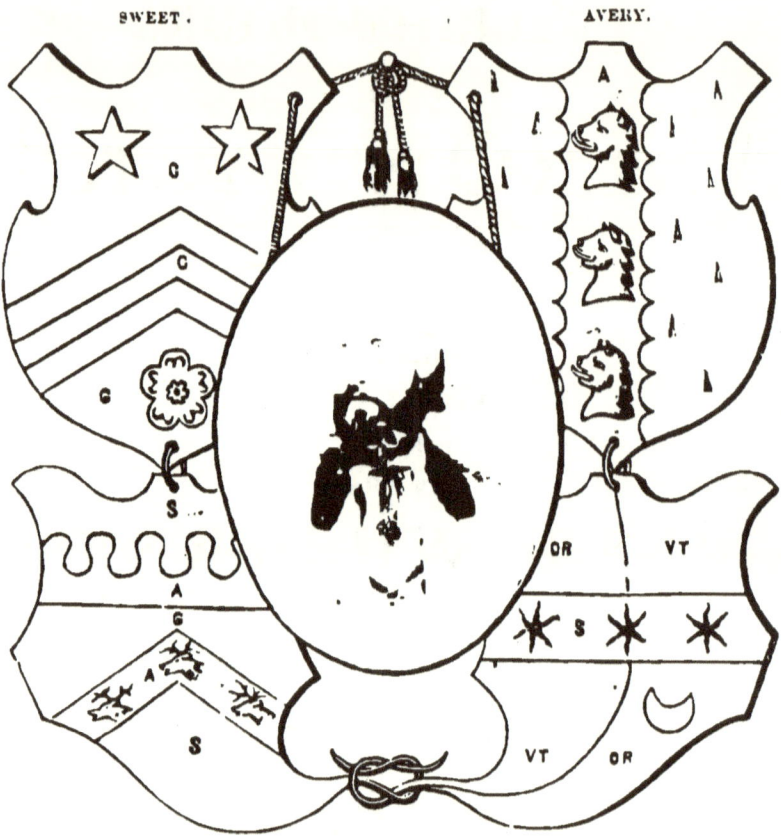

Entered according to Act of Congress in the year 1870, by

Homer D. L. Sweet,

In the Clerk's Office of the District Court of the United States, for the Northern District of New York.

HITCHCOCK & SMITH,
PRINTERS,
SYRACUSE, N. Y.

DUNHAM & RUSSELL,
BINDERS,
20 NORTH WILLIAM ST., N. Y.

DEDICATION.

TO MRS. C. B. M.,

Who, in my boyish days, was the first to discover in me the little spark of poetic merit, and who has been my chief counselor in this literary undertaking, as a feeble acknowledgment of the deep debt of gratitude I owe her, this little volume is respectfully inscribed.

CONTENTS.

The subjects will be found following the line designated by the number in the table.

CHAPTER I. THE PROFESSOR.

1, Chronicle. 121, LECTURE: Cosmogony; 157, Mountains, Geology and Mineralogy; 229, Lakes; 295, Rivers; 337, Geological Progress; 355, Forests; 385, Natural History; 421, Chronicle. 469, TRADITION: 500, The Captive and Maiden; 577, The Flight and Home; 649, The Marriage and Hermit Life; 721, Children and Courtships; 769, Chronicle.—792.

CHAPTER II. THE TRAVELER.

1, Chronicle. 67, SHELLS OF RIVERS: St. Lawrence, Genesee, Thames, Tweed, Avon; 148, Shakspeare's Tomb; 233, River of Life. 386, SHELLS OF LAKES: Skaneateles, Racket, Erie; 413, Nameless Grave; 461, Swiss Lakes, Scottish Lakes; 488, Highland Beauty. 565, SHELLS OF OCEAN: 704, Youth; 752, Early Manhood; 800, Manhood's Prime; 850, Old Age; 910, Chronicle.—963

CHAPTER III. THE POET.

1, Chronicle. 97, THE DREAM: 193, Minerva; 249, Poet's Fate; 373, Æolus; 409, The Winds; 649, Jupiter's Proclamation; 811, Apollo; 837, Crowning Song; 861, Finale; 893, Chronicle.—960.

CHAPTER IV. THE ENGINEER.

1, Chronicle. 67, IRON ORE: 93, Age of Stone; 171, Discovery of Iron; 223, The Smith; 249, Iron Age; 275, Age of Steel; 301, Inventions; 325, Fiction; 353, Imagination. 379, LAY OF A LU-

I.

Contents.

NATIC: Sunset; 438, Aurora Borealis; 595, Electricity; 727, The Journey, Neptune, Uranus, Jupiter, Saturn; 811, Juno; 849, Mars; 872, Venus; 897, Mercury; 921, Luna; 961, Finale; 1,004, Chronicle.—1,028.

CHAPTER V. THE HISTORIAN.

1, Chronicle. 19, NICHOLAS' TRADITION OF THE MOHAWKS: The Boston Tea Party; 223, Samuel Adams' Speech; 295, Conclusion. 319, GRANDFATHER'S STORY OF THE CAPTURE OF TICONDEROGA; 507, Interlude. 554, CÆSAR'S NARRATIVE OF THE RAID OF JOHN BROWN: 602, John Brown's Speech; 758, Conclusion. 794, SAM'S STORY OF SUMTER. 996, Chronicle.—1,018.

CHAPTER VI. THE HUMORIST.

1, Chronicle. 43, PANEGYRIC ON MIRTH. 231. PUTTING ON AIRS. 571, BOARDING AROUND: 638, Jones' Liver; 679, Schneider's Cheese; 711, McVey's Respect; 763, Perry's Gander; 797, Poor but Proud; 842, The Village; 865, Widow Blake, Imogene, Courtship and Happy Conclusion; 988, Chronicle.—1,012.

CHAPTER VII. THE FARMER.

1, Chronicle. 43, Farmer's Apology; 127, January; 199, February; 271, March; 343, April; 415, May; 487, June; 559, July; 631, August; 703, September; 775, October; 847, November; 919, December; 991, Chronicle.—1,014.

CHAPTER VIII. CHOWDER.

1, Chronicle; 31, The Gold Hunter; 111, Old Bachelor; 203, Beautiful Eyes; 249, Poe and Annabel Lee; 297, District School House; 343, Ricketty Stile; 405, The Declaration; 475, Mary Blake; 509, O-ra-la Loo; 569, Young Folks from Home; 607, Native Hills; 645, O-ri-o-la Loo-lee; 681, Song of the Engineer; 727, Chains of Memory; 748, Excuses; 800, Boys in Blue; 845, Nature's Music; 893, Old John Brown; 955, Good Night.—990.

II.

INTRODUCTION.

(Circular.)

Pompey, N. Y., June 1, 1868.

My Dear Fellow :—

I should be happy to have you join a party of friends, to spend a month in the wilds of the Adirondacks for scientific investigation, physical recuperation, and mental recreation.

Will you come prepared to entertain the party one evening, at least, on the subject which you consider your own peculiar province?

All the minor necessaries,—transportation, provisions, guides, and so forth,—will be faithfully attended to by myself; and you will be expected at Crown Point on the the tenth of August next.

Truly yours,   Homer D. L. Sweet.

The following extracts from favorable replies need no explanation farther than to say that each man was faithfully on hand at the appointed time :—

"Granite Hall," June 4th, 1868.

*   *   *   *   Scientific knowledge should lie at the bottom of all earthly pleasure. Each superadded strata of intellectual attainment should rise like the various epochs in Geological history, and finally be crowned with the alluvial deposits rich in all the elements of instruction.

I will be there in time and add my little cobble to your cairn—

Truly yours,   "Mica Schist."

Introduction.

"MINE OYSTER," June 5th, 1868.

* * * * Nothing would suit me better than a trip to that *terra incognita*.

I shall expect to gather shells enough to complete my belt of wampum, from which I will make liberal translations, if occasion should require.

As ever, yours, "CRAWFISH."

"PARNASSUS," June 6th, 1868.

* * * * Your flattering invitation to visit that land of "fable and fiction" almost overwhelms me, and I accept it with pleasure.

I cannot pledge myself to entertain you, but presume the atmosphere will invigorate my fervor, the scenery will enliven my fancy, and the cheering presence of congenial friends exhilarate my feelings enough to produce something worthy of the occasion.

Very respectfully yours, "POETA."

"IN THE FIELD," 6, 7, '68.

* * * * My health has run off on a tangent, and is now going on a down grade at the rate of 40 miles per hour. If it is not switched off pretty soon at a side station to recruit, there will be a collapse. My boiler ought to be cleaned, and the soft water of that region certainly should do it.

I have nothing on hand to read to you. I may have time before then to do something, but shall trust to my getting up steam after my boiler is overhauled, and try to invent something.

As ever, thine, "ENGINEER."

IV.

Introduction.

"LIBRARY HALL," June 8th, '68,

* * * * I shall be delighted to join the expedition, but I fear I can do nothing in my own line worthy of note. All I have written has been printed, except a scrap on "Ticonderoga," which would not occupy over fifteen minutes, and I shall have to trust to luck for more material, as "history is not invented."

As ever, always, "PLUTARCH."

"LAUGH-E-YET," June 10, 1868.

Dear Sacharissa :—Your *(Circular)* letter, which was " on the square," although received on the second, could not be read until to-day, *(*to allow it time to open its eyes*)*, and in reply, I venture to hint that such an arrangement would suit me to a T. In May last I blossomed, *(*I always blow in May*)*, and I have carefully preserved the blossom in my Herbarium. I call it " Putting on Airs," with which, and some other old matter, I think I can make an hour tedious. I will close school and come.

"SMARTWEED."

REPAIRS.

CHAPTER I: Line 252, *fondled* in place of caught ; 486, omit third *the*. Chap. II: 166, omit *my ;* 340, " charm" ; 401, " every hope." Chap. III: 246, " The gods approving" ; 855, *marland*—a loose braid ; 931, " blends" ; 937, " brute." Chap. IV : 516, *fiddle* —a trifle ; 583, *gnomen*—a female gnome. Chap. V : 313, " teachest's." Chap. VI : 316, supplied by a classical friend ; 496, omit *the ;* 538, omit second *a ;* 874, *her* in place of first " wish" ; 906, " France" ; 954, " was most." Chap. VII : 483, " grotto 's" ; 495, " brook" ; 696, " fifteen" ; 895, " floor" ; 896, " right" ; 1,011, " rivers." Chap. VIII : 153, " boots" ; 183, " Where" ; 480, "and I."

V.

CHAPTER I.

THE PROFESSOR.

Chronicle.

OUR camp is made on Opalescent River,
   Just where a little branch comes in from Colden,
These meet, embrace, and fairly seem to quiver
   With fresh delight, within the glorious, golden
Sunlight, that tinges every wave with amber,
In imitation of a naiad's chamber.

The stream is small—some thirty feet—not wider,
   And moves 'mid many maple-sugary stones,
With just the flash and color of boiled cider,—
   Its ripples giving out in faintest tones,
The sweetest music, with the gentlest motion,
That soothes the senses like lethean potion.

Our cabin, partly made by two huge boulders,
   Whose moss-grown sides give many a varied hue,
Though rough, is higher than a tall man's shoulders;
   The third side, logs piled carefully and true;
The fourth is open,—this we all love dearly,—
It gives a prospect to the south-west clearly.

The Professor.

The roof is bark of spruce, peeled from the trunks,
    And gives balsamic odors to the air;
The smudge in front, built of decaying chunks,
    Sends up its curling wreaths like incense rare,
And drives from us the gnats, flies and musketoes,
Much more effectual than bars and vetoes.

Before this parlor cabin, twelve by twenty,
    On rustic seats, or lounging on log couches,
Are grouped my friends, for this occasion plenty,
    Who, late returned, are emptying their pouches,
Their bags and baskets, for they each have hoarded
Some wealth the hills or rivers have afforded.

They all have game, replenishing our larder,—
    Two squirrels and a rabbit, fat and tender,
Four fine black duck with coarser flesh, and harder,
    A crane, (for stuffing), with long legs and slender;
Some forty speckled beauties from the brook,
And caught, as all are, by a treacherous hook.

The guide, Sam D——, a broad and brawny fellow,
    Has killed a buck, "still-hunting" on the hill;
His partner, Nick, half Indian, slightly yellow,
    Is helping him to dress it with a will;
While Cæsar stands, a handsome, bright quadroon,
And merely looks,—a lazy, lounging loon.

Chronicle.

These friends of mine, and I, the mythic seven,
   Have been a week within this rustic hall,—
This painter's paradise, this poet's heaven,
   And palace of Aladdin for us all;
For each has gained from mountain, lake or rock,
A contribution to the common stock.

The first brings opals fit for a coronet,
   The second, tiny shells, pearl, purple, pink;
The third, a poem,—some grand scene he's met;
   The fourth, rich iron ore, as black as ink;
The fifth, a tale told by a volunteer;
The sixth, rare funny-dotes, and stories queer.

Around the room in admirable confusion,
   The satchels, bags, game, guns and fishing rods,
With clothing hang in plentiful profusion.
   Upon the table, are the ends and odds
Of our last meal, which we have just concluded,—
'T was tea and toast, with several jokes included.

We have another house we call the kitchen,
   Behind this one, where Cæsar does the cooking,—
Where dogs and guides promiscuously pitch in
   To sleep at night, unless they 're out a-looking
Upon Lake Sanford, for some old buck, silly,
That feeds and fattens on the water lily.

The Professor.

"Come, Cæsar, come!" *(The writer does the calling),*
 "Clear up the table, put away the dishes,
Then take these trout to where the brook is brawling,
 For we must have a breakfast of those fishes;
And hurry some, you can't be weary walking,
Then fix the fire, we're going to have some talking."

While he those several orders is obeying,—
 The parlor placing in its best attire,—
My friends aside attractive things are laying,
 For all, save one, have curious desire
To hear the speaker and to learn his power;
But ere I introduce him, mark the hour.

'T is twilight hour; the sun has just descended
 Into that notch between two rugged mountains;
The last rays, lingering, kiss the unoffended
 Rill as it blushes. Two of the sweetest fountains
That burst in beauty from the bluff behind us,
Of laughing, dancing, chattering girls remind us.

All else is still, the hum of insects hushed;
 The rippled river gives no gentle sighing;
No tree-top quivers, by the breezes brushed,
 And e'en the music of the rill is dying.
A sleepy stillness fills the atmosphere,
As though the world was hushed by sudden fear.

Chronicle.

The sky above is bare, and broad and blue,
  No cloud is there to mar or beautify it;
Around the horizon lies in creamy hue,
  A fading belt, save where the sunbeams dye it;
Below, the grand old mountains intervene,
All clothed in garments of perpetual green.

The speaker is a student in the sciences,
  Not getting learning merely from the books,
But studying nature, using all appliances
  Within his reach, in earnest search, and looks
For all things useful, from the simplest grasses,
To the most mighty of the mountain masses.

He talks quite easily upon geography,
  And gives a little sprinkling of geology,—
Is master of this wilderness chorography,
  And shows at least a zeal for rare zoology,
Beside a smattering of mineralogy,
And a slight taste for tracing genealogy.

We call him here, "Professor," though his knowledge
  Was not obtained in any of the schools
That have high-sounding names, or any college,
  Save Universities where Nature rules;
But, from the modest, humblest, underrated
Old District School, it was, he graduated.

I.

The Professor.

His age, perhaps, two score, *(*I only guess*)*,
   For off his roof old Time has pulled the thatch;
His gray eye smiling boyish, ne'ertheless,
   With full brown beard and light mustache to match.
He speaks in tones like an old Grecian teaching,—
So slow, so sweet, 't is very much like preaching.

LECTURE.

Cosmogony.

My friends, but a few days ago we were perched on
   the top of Mount Marcy;
The North, in its limit of vision, was bounded by
   noble St. Lawrence;
Champlain, far away in the East, only shone in the
   smallest of patches;
The South, overwhelmed in the smoke that arose from
   the burning of forests;
The West by some dark, rolling clouds, so portent-
   ous of showers and thunder;—
A scene to be viewed and remembered through life, to
   its latest of moments.

Lecture—Cosmogony.

The air so ethereally thin, clear and calm, and so
   keen in its coldness,
That half of our ardor was gone ere we gained the
   first sight from the summit.
We gazed in such mute admiration, o'er all of the
   beauties surrounding,
In haste to record in our minds, every feature of
   glory and grandeur,
That longer we could not remain,—there I could
   not deliver my lecture;
But now I will read, though its force is half lost in
   its non-application.

Far back in that age of the world, but a day since the
   dawn of creation,
The fiat went forth from Jehovah, dividing the land
   from the water;
The earth in her labor convulsed, groaned aloud in
   her terrible anguish,
And ocean tumultuously rolled, as though swept by
   the breath of a tempest;
Mount Marcy arose on the wave, but a barren and
   desolate island;
Ta-haw-us, the sky-splitting rock, was alone the di-
   vider of oceans.

Around him and washing his borders, the waves were
   incessantly dashing;

The Professor.

But, slowly receding, he saw them upspringing to birth through the surges,—
His brothers and sisters arising and dashing the foam from their foreheads,—
He welcomed each birth in the group, with a smile of serene satisfaction;
The waves in their musical swell, wed the winds in a jubilant chorus,
Till hundreds were joined in the group, like a monarch surrounded by courtiers.

For ages and ages they stood, with the waves still surrounding their bases,
And washing the rocks from their sides, that were tumbled and rolled into boulders.
At length all their bases united, save where in the deepest of valleys,
Some lakelet lay smiling asleep, and reflected the stars like a mirror,
Or river went rippling along, or the brooks babbling over the pebbles,
That gave to each brother his share, yet concealing the bond of their union.

These mountains in clusters and groups, now are forming five principal ranges,
That lie in irregular lines, far across the Great Wilderness country.

Lecture—Mountains.

The prominent feature in each, and a good one in every landscape;
They loom up so grand in the distance, serrating the pinkish horizon,
Or nearer, impress us with awe, as they rise in their beauty so mighty,
O'erwhelming the mind, as it were, in its effort to grasp at their greatness. 159

Mountains.

The first of these ranges is longest and highest,—the grand Adirondack,—
That lies in a double waved line from Champlain far away to the Mohawk,
Dissevered but slightly in course, by the chance intervention of valleys,
But broken, distorted, and torn into families, clusters and masses
Most mighty, sublimely majestic, when viewed in the light of their vastness,—
Each simple, impressive and grand, like a volume of Dramas by Shakspeare.

The rocks in this range are peculiar; the most, if not all, are volcanic.
I. 163

The Professor.

First, Hypersthone gray, flecked and spotted, with
green intermixed, dull and smoky,
Is found in three-fourths of its length, but without
either system or order.
Next, Gneiss, and then Granite appears, with occa-
sional primitive limestone;
While Porphyry, Serpentine, Trap, beside Sienite,
Steatite, Hornblende,
Add beauty to every variety, making the whole inter-
esting.

Of minerals useful to all men, the most so we find
here, is iron,
Abounding in wonderful masses; immense beds and
veins are abundant;
Of this there alone is enough within five miles, at
most, of our cabin,
To build for the world all the railroads that are or
will ever be needed.
The graphite is frequently found, and galena in plen-
ty of places,
While traces of copper and silver await the researches
of science.

The minerals rare, and the gems, here are often abun-
dant and brilliant;
The augite, the garnet, and zircon; the epidote, chlo-
rite and jasper.

Lecture—Mountains.

Refulgent in lustre and beauty, and hanging in caves like stalactites;
The coccolite, sphene, adularian, sahlite, rose-spar and carnelian,
In ledges and crystalline grottoes, or mighty calcareous masses,
That vie in their beauty and value, with caskets of Indian Princes.

The mountains that lie to the south,—the remaining four principal ranges,—
Are broken, dissevered, and torn by the mighty convulsions of nature,
With many more lateral spurs running out from their axes erratic,
With valleys, deep cleft, intersecting their bases so broad and substantial;
Their sides sadly scarred by the brooks that come down from the summits well rounded,
Save here and there one, like a chieftain, with lofty and conical apex.

The first of these four, the Boquet range, is lofty, and lengthy, and crooked,
And broad, with a plenty of prominent peaks; but the principal, Dix's,
That looms up so sharply and stately, a chieftan above his companions.

The Professor.

The second, the Schroon range, distorted and broken
 in jumbled confusion,
So scattered in groups, and in isolate masses, 't is
 difficult tracing
Continuous peaks, but of many, Mount Crane is ac-
 knowledged the leader.

The Ka-ya-de-ros-e-ras next, is not nearly as long as
 the others,—
Confined more in breadth and in hight; more contin-
 uous far in its outline;
More graceful the curves on its flanks, like an army
 commanded by Pharaoh.
The fourth, last and lowest of all, but best known as
 the Palmerton Mountains,
Lies far to the east, and surrounded, or nearly, by
 bodies of water,—
Almost a continuous ridge, well deserving the name
 of Sierra.

The rock of these ranges is gneiss, with a little of
 crystalline limestone;
Gray granite but seldom appears, and the Potsdam
 red sandstone is lacking;
Calciferous sand rock is rare, but the Chazy, the
 Trenton and Birdseye,
Are limestones that lie on the lake, but with limits
 both little and local.

Lecture—Mountains.

In minerals useful and rare we've no doubt they are
rich and prolific,
But, saving the graphite and iron, none others have
taken attention.

Afar to the north of us lie surely fifty lone peaks
high and noble,
That, scattered in wildest disorder for leagues
through this wilderness region,
Seem lifted up out of the plateau in couplets, or triplets, or singly;
For earth, at the time they were born, was of mountains most wondrous prolific.
Mount Seward, and Emmons, and Lyon, St. Regis,
and Moosehead, and Whiteface,
And dozens and dozens of others, though nameless,
are worthy of notice.

The glory, the beauty of mountains, when viewed
from the depths of the valleys,
They rise in their infinite might, and transfixing the
bosom of ether,
Their conical summits enshrouded with clouds pale
and pure as a spirit,
And shoulders broad, brawny and bare, save a mantle
of mosses and lichens,
And bases surrounded with forests, thus hiding their
rough imperfections,

The Professor.

Seem light from the darkness upspringing—sublimity rising from grandeur.

When viewed from a prominent summit with hundreds of peaks lying round it,
Like waves of the ocean in tumult, congealed in their awful commotion;
With lakes in the valleys between, that reflect the rich hues of the sunset,
Like jewels that flash in the hair of a young Ethiopian beauty;
Where rivers and brooks intervene, wind and turn in their tortuous courses,
Like ribbons of silver and gold, that are wafted and swayed by the breezes.

The soul in such scenery as this, is elastic and light as the ether,—
Seems longing to leap from the earth and alight in the blue empyrean.
If proud of its noble attainments, and aiming at higher and nobler,
Rejoices in anticipation of honors and glories to crown it;
Contemplating self, it can see all its littleness, infinite smallness,
And learning to look upon Nature, appreciate Infinite Greatness.

Lecture—Lakes.

Lakes.

The lakes that lie deep in the vales of this wild and romantic dominion,
Are grand in their beauty and size,—in variety great, and in number;
As deep and as dark as the tarns that were sung of by Sagas of Iceland;
As bright and as blue as the lochs that are praised by the poets of Scotland;
As varied in contour and size as the meres of Helvetia, historic;
As flashing and free in the breezes as were ever Italy's Lagos.

Commence with the largest: Lake George is romantic in every feature,—
Irregular, broad, deep and blue, and the water cold, clear, pure as ether,
The shore torn and ragged with rocks, where the waves are monotonous dashing;
Or coves fringed with soft, sandy beaches, and ripples continuously laughing;
The islands that fleck its fair bosom, though lavishly scattered and broken,
(As ponds, little gems in a forest,) add charms, as do dimples to beauty.

The Professor.

The rocks that rise up from the shore, are reflected in truth in its bosom,—
Not truer the gem lapis lazuli gives to the eye back its brightness.
The gorges, the glens and the dales, on their sides so secluded and shady,
Your fancy could people with fawns, or with fairies, or sylvans or satyrs;
The serpentine grottoes of green can as well be the birth-place of naiads,
As crystalline caverns and groves in the waves of the sea of the Grecian.

The fine sandy beaches, with pebbles and shells intermixed in profusion,
In ridges so handsomely curved, and assorted in regular sizes,
So soft to the foot that's unshod, that it yields like an Indian carpet.
The ripples that play at your feet that are bared to be bathed by their motion,
Reach farther and farther, coquetting, or laughingly play round your ankles,
Like children that want to be caught, yet flee if you're trying to catch them.

The islands are bright little emeralds, set in cerulean splendor,

Lecture—Lakes.

Like gems from the crown of a prince who has met
  with destructive disaster,
And strewn on the floor of a palace in natural, wondrous confusion ;
They 've every shadow of green that the forest can give, or the grasses,
Have every hue in the rocks, from the ruby to blackest of boulder,—
The chief of its glories, the crown, as the soul gives to woman her beauty.

In all of the principal valleys dividing these ridges of mountains,
Large lakes lie, as wondrous in beauty as Como, Luzerne, or Loch Lomond,
In all of their minor relations, in all of their local surroundings,—
The woodland, the hill-side, the rocks, and the mountains that notch the horizon.
'T is only where snow-covered peaks in the distance can lend their enchantment,
Is scenery more beautif'ly grand than is here in the Old Adirondacks.

South-east lie the Brant and the Schroon; then the Indian, Pleasant, Piseco.
South-west is the long chain of Fulton, the Racket, the Forked, and Eckford.

The Professor.

Due west is the Long Lake, two Tuppers, Smith's,
    Chase's, the great Oswegatchie.
The Saranacs lying north-west, with the Jordan be-
    yond, and St. Regis.
North, Meacham and Ragged, and Loon, with the
    two Chateaugays, and the Chazy,
And near to the base of old Whiteface lies one of the
    finest, Lake Placid.

To give but a list of the smaller, assign them appro-
    priate places,
To tell of the beauty and brightness that lies in this
    desert of forest,
That scarcely is seen save by stars that have watched
    them and bathed in them nightly;
That, nameless, abound in this region, and known
    unto none, or not many,
Would occupy much of my time, and consume far
    too much of your patience,—
A task scarcely equaled by Homer's, in naming the
    fleets of the Trojans.

Delightfully beautiful lakes! When a gale sweeping
    over your bosoms,—
Makes white the wild waves, and they dance all so joy-
    fully, loving, coquetting,
Now up and then down, in and out, here and there,
    now advancing, retreating,

Till, reaching the shore, they are dashed on the rocks,
and in sudden destruction,
More beautiful far to the eye, to the ear all too harsh
and discordant,
Like hearts that are struggling with fate, yet will
laugh at their own dissolution.

Deliciously charming the lakelet that lies in an emerald setting,—
As dark and as bright as the flash of the eye of a lady
of Cadiz;
As silent as sleep, for the ripple just breaks, as it were,
on its border.
So deep, and yet into its darkness the vision of man
cannot enter;
Reflecting alone from its surface, the beauties that
hover around it,—
A heart overwhelmed in its sadness, reflecting the
gladness of others.

The mind, when contemplating lakes that are lying
in forest recesses,
Begins to grow sad and reserved, when the first flush
of transport is over.
When looking down into their depths, as though
looking far into the future,
All dreary and dim is the darkness, all vague are the
vistas that vanish

The Professor.

Before the keen gaze of the soul that is longing and
  looking for brightness,—
A star, faint and feeble, appears,—the reflection of
  one in the heavens.

Rivers.

The rivers that rise in this region, and flow to all
  points of the compass,
Are numerous, lengthy, and large, interlocked in
  their tiniest sources,
Like branches of trees intertwined, labyrinthian-like
  in their mazes,
That vex the chorographer much, in his efforts to
  trace them distinctly.
They flow in long, tortuous courses, in deepest and
  narrowest valleys,—
In reaches of quiet and stillness, or dashed into foam
  in the rapids.

The first on the north, is the Indian Branch, then the
  main Oswegatchie,
The Grass and the Racket, St. Regis, the Salmon, the
  Chateaugay, Chazy,
The Saranac, Salmon, Ausable, the Boquet, the
  Schroon, and the Hudson;

Lecture—Rivers.

The wild Sacandaga, and others, that take the long
    route to the Mohawk.
The Black, and the Beaver, and Moose, that depart
    for Ontario basin;
All these, and as many beside, you will find if you
    search in the circle.

The rills and the brooks whose rare sources are found
    near the summits of mountains,
In springs cold and pure as the sky on the frostiest
    night in November,—
They trickle, and drizzle, and babble, and brawl in
    the gullies of pebbles;
They rattle, and rumble, and roar in their beds
    among brawniest boulders,
Till filled by the melting of snow, and then swollen
    by heaviest showers,
Unitedly form in their strength the beginning of
    some mighty river.

The Racket, the longest and largest that flows to the
    mighty St. Lawrence,
Whose source is a lake of rare beauty, and lies higher
    far than its fellows,
With beautiful headlands, and bays that extend way
    up into the valleys,
To catch ev'ry creek as it wanders away from its
    home in the mountains,

The Professor.

And bear in the depth of its bosom the crystalline flood in its brightness,
Away to the valley below, and away to the limitless ocean.

All marshaled its forces from every quarter, it speeds to the rapids,
Where, broken and torn by the rocks that arise, and, disputing its passage,
It turns to the right or the left, and is dashed here and there against boulders;
In eddying whirls, flecked with foam, fairly mad in its vexing confusion,
The barriers leaping, and tossing its fragments of spray on the margin,—
Rests quiet and calm in the pool, or reluctantly goes on its journey.

So sadly, so slowly, so sleepily winding its way to the ocean;
As dark, and as deep, and as drear as the Styx, in the regions infernal.
You float on the current, and almost imagine the ferryman, Charon,
Is going to hail you from battlement high, of a rocky old castle;
Then swinging around through the forest, in densest of shadowing darkness,

Lecture—Geology.

Again turn and gather new force, and again rushes
   on to a cascade.

How like to the River of Life are those streams that
   arise so obscurely,
Like delicate children, too slender, too small to be'
   noticed or useful,
Increasing in size, they go dashing, impetuous youth,
   full of passion,
Till civilization in manhood puts on them the harness of labor;
Exhausted on reaching the valleys, bear burdens
   along on their bosoms,
And quietly, silent, and sober, sink into oblivious
   ocean.

Geology.

Geologists tell us, you know, and the records they
   have we rely on,
'T was ages and ages ago, when the elements worked
   on the mountain,
That rain, and the frost, and the snow were dissolving
   the gneiss and the granite,
And into the valleys below rolled the boulders, and
   cobbles, and pebbles,

And ground them exceedingly slow, into sand intermixed with the masses,—
Gave footing where lichens could grow, and then, perishing, add to its humus.

The sea weeds, and mosses, and grasses then grew in the lakes in the valleys,
Without either orders or classes, or genera, species, or number.
Above in the intricate passes and gorges, the ferns were abundant,
And clinging to great rocky masses, were low-trailing vines in profusion;
And deep in the dankest morasses, the rushes luxuriant flourished,—
Their record, enduring as brass is, you read in the layers of limestone.

From these and their gradual decay, was a soil for superior species;
The hardier shrubs, and the plants, and the vines climbing up on their branches;
The larches, and spruces, and balsams; the cedars, the pines and the hemlocks;
The maples, and beeches, and birches; the oaks, and the elms, and the chestnuts;
The hickory, butternut, cherry, with ironwood, dogwood and basswood,

Lecture—Forests.

With several species of most, and some others that
botanists mention.

Forests.

The forests that cover the valleys, have grandeur in
every feature;
The huge but symmetrical trunks, that arise like Corinthian columns,
Form long but irregular aisles in the grandest of Nature's Cathedrals;
The branches in arches above, join in every species
of gothic,—
The circular, pointed, or waved, with their ornaments
beautiful, graceful,
With evergreens clustered between, like a church
decorated for Christmas.

The flowers, the brambles and shrubs, and the vines
in their richest profusion,
So seemingly hide from our vision the thousands of
worshipers, kneeling;
The mighty and moss-covered boulder, a pulpit in
eloquent silence,
That preaches those "sermons in stones," which are
read but not heeded by mortals;

The Professor.

The deep, roaring river beyond, in a volume of sound
    diastaltic,
That rises and falls on the zephyr in tones richer far
    than the organ.

On hillside, or mountain, above where the beeches
    and maples can flourish,
And evergreens, dark in their density, stand like a
    band of young brothers,
In aiding each other to live, by protecting the earth
    in its moisture,
Assisting each other to stand when the hurricane
    sweeps o'er their foreheads;
Affording the choicest of shade that is filled with a
    native perfumery,
Ambrosial, seductive, and soothing, so fitting for
    moods of reflection.

And higher, where spruces grow stinted, and bram-
    bles, and ferns, and coarse grasses
Are scattered in limited patches, with mosses and
    rocks intervening,
More sterile, more scattered, more stinted, till all
    vegetation has vanished.
Look back on the forest behind you; the green in its
    various tinges,
The mass of mankind no more varied, the tops seem-
    ing even, completely,

Lecture—Natural History.

Except an occasional pine, like a poet, o'ertopping
  his fellows.

The soul that is joyous on mountains, is sobered and
  sad in the valleys.
The soul that would worship in temples, in solitude
  seeks contemplation.
The mind that expands with the scene, and can grasp
  at a glance the whole landscape,
Can stoop to the frailest of flowers, and gather some
  silent instruction.
The heart that is broken and lonely, makes sweetest
  of tones in its anguish,
Like trees snapped asunder by tempests, when breezes
  but breathe on the splinters.

Natural History.

In progress of time, we assume that here animate nature assembled;
The birds built their nests in the forests, and have
  since their day of creation;
The elk, and the moose, and the deer, roamed both
  fearless and free on the hillside;
The panther, the wolf, and the bear, made their haunts
  in the mountain recesses,

While nearer the river and lake lived the otter, the martin and beaver;
And these, clear and cold, in abundance were stocked with most beautiful fishes.

The eagle, the king of the birds, built his home on a crag of the mountain,
And viewed, from his eyrie exalted, his broad and delightful dominion.
The hawk, and the owl, and the raven, the crow, and the blackbird, and partridge,
And others, the wild woodland warblers, made homes in the spring-time and summer;
The crane, and the loon, and king-fisher had haunts in the margins of marshes,
That lie 'round the rivers and lakes, where the wild duck was breeding, contented.

The moose, here the largest of quadrupeds, roamed through the forest in freedom,
His antlers majestic thrown back on his shoulders, his nostrils dilated,
He dashes from danger, through forests, o'er mountains, and wades through morasses,
Defying pursuit of the foe, and, excepting when snow-banks surround him,
Succeeds; but in these stands at bay, with an aspect terrific, defiant,

His roar in the mountains resounds, till he dies, like
a hero in battle.

The engineer, architect beaver, erected his dam and
his dwelling,
With instinct allied to mankind, but not hardly pos-
sessing his reason.
The skill, the sagacity used, with the forethought for
food in the winter;
His house, so secure from attacks of all prowling
carniverous creatures;
His dam, that could stand in a freshet that furnished
a transport for timber
Whose bark he must chiefly subsist on, all mark him
the wonder of nature.

The fishes that swarmed in these streams, and in lakes
in the greatest profusion,
(Whose flesh, so deliciously delicate, we are so often
regaled on),
In species were many and rarest; but noblest of all
was the salmon.
The trout, still so plentiful here in its beauty, in lake,
brook, or river;
The shad made their annual migrations; the pickerel,
bass, and the sturgeon,
And others as worthy of mention.   I close, ere I
weary your patience.

The Professor.

A red man, the first in these wilds, in pursuit of an
  otter or beaver,
And clothed in the skins of wild beasts, only armed
  with a bow and an arrow ;
Enchanted with beauty and wealth, was so awed with
  its terrible grandeur,
His voice in spontaneous praises went upward to
  thank the Great Spirit.
This vision, so real to him, of a land he would find
  in hereafter,
He named it, we hope for all time, Adirondack,—the
  Indian's Heaven.

Chronicle.

The speaker ceases, and the friends around him,
  Of course, make comments on the wondrous skill
That he's displayed.   The guide Sam, thinks he'll
  sound him,
  And asks a dozen questions of some hill
(That he terms "mountain,") that he once ascended.
He finds him "sound," and so his queries ended.

The Indian, who has paid most strict attention
  To every word the Lecturer has spoken,
Speaks, as he says, "without the least intention

Chronicle.

To bring discredit, or have fancy broken;
The lecture, like a mountain, can't be shaken,
Except the close,—the speaker is mistaken.

" The Indian who first found this little heaven,
As it has been transmitted down to me,
Was not out hunting, no, nor fishing even,
But captive unto one,—to all else free.
If all desire, I 'll give a fair rendition,
And truthful, of our family tradition."

" Proceed, proceed," says each man in the shanty;
"Nothing, of course, just now could please us
better;"
Of these traditions histories are so scanty,
We 'll try and save it, faithful to the letter.
" If you 'll speak slowly, so that I can write it,
We 'll have it printed just as you recite it."

Now, Nick, the guide, is quite a handsome fellow,
The Saxon blood just blossoms in his cheek;
His eye is mild; most musically mellow
Is his soft voice; we love to hear him speak,
It rings so bell-like, and his language jinglish,
That sounds about half Indian and half English.

Though born within the darkest forest shade,
He's had the aid of civilized society;

The Professor.

Has been to school, to church, and progress made
   In many graces, talks with strict propriety;
Would fill with dignity a higher station,
And never yet disgraced his white relation.

He knows the history of St. Regis tribe,
   And many of their legends and traditions;
Each, in his way, minutely can describe,—
   The rites they practiced, and the superstitions
That governed them in all their hopes and fears,
Back in their darkness many hundred years.

There is a mixture in his composition,
   Like ancient Chibiabos and Iagoo.
As one, is both a poet and musician;
   As story teller seldom lets the day go
Without repeating some delightful story;
Then, as the other, revels in his glory.

Tradition.

When the snow on the mountain top gathers once
   more,
It will number two hundred exact, and six tens,
Since the Iroquois Indians met on Champlain
The Algonquins, their enemies ancient and brave;
Where a terrible battle was fought on the shore,

Tradition.

And they first saw a white man, and first heard a gun.
A young chief of the Mohawks was first to be harmed;
A blue bullet had hit him and broken his arm,
So, he being unable to fight, tried to flee,
And unconsciously fainting, was captured and bound.
When the conflict was over, (the Mohawks had fled),
The Algonquins returned to their homes at Quebec
With the captives they'd taken, a dozen or more;
Some were subject to torture, some died, some escap'd,
But this chief was so closely confined that he found
It impossible, maimed as he was, to succeed,
And in quiet submitted to fate, should it come
In the shape of the torture, or the ransomed release.
 Here, the surgeons who came in the ships with the whites,
Put his arm in the stocks; he was saved from the stake
In the hope that the tribe of which he was a chief,
Would, in time, give a ransom; the Mohawks were rich,
And had corn in great plenty, and wampum of shells.
 In dividing the spoil, it so fell to the lot
Of this chief, that the tribe of St. Francis drew him,
And they paddled away many days up the stream,
Where the three mighty rivers are lost in the one.
He was guarded securely by day, and at night
He was bound in addition, with sinews of deer
Round his ankles and wrists, and all these to a tree.

The Professor.

With a very strong cabin erected around.
Every day at its dawn, every day at its close,
Came a maiden with food, and so nicely prepared,
Which she gave him to eat, while she loosened the bonds
That encumbered his wrists, and she looked to the arm
That was maimed, and she wet it with water,—with tears.
It is true that she loosened the bonds on his limbs,
But she bound him in bands that were stronger than steel;
And if every sinew of deer had been dropped
From his limbs, and he'd then been informed he was free,
He'd have stayed; for he could not, he would not depart.
 In the night she would steal to his prison, so still
That none knew she was there, and in whispers they talked
Of his home o'er the hills, of his parents and friends,
And she sought in the simplest of ways, if his heart
Had been tangled with love,—if some maiden at home
Had not cast her dark eye into his, and she strove
But to make him acknowledge some sweetheart, some love
That yet lingered and fluttered around his poor heart.
 But he would not admit that the fairest of fair

Tradition.

That had fluttered before him, and dazzled his eye,
Made the slightest impression upon his soft heart.
Now he knew the full worth of a woman; he felt
The full power of her pity, her sympathy, love,
And he bowed in his weakness; her kindness had won
From his lips what ought not to be told. It was death
To them both should they wed;—he a captive and
    bound,
She the daughter and heir of a chief, and their tribes
Still at war; could they move that great mountain
    with love?
It was death if they wed not, and death if they did;
They embraced; he was faint; she departed and wept.
    Did she love the young chieftain unwisely, or well?
Was it sympathy, merely? or pity, or love?
These are questions she asked of herself, and each time
There came back the same answer, "I love and he
    loves."
Then a fear seized her mind, and she thought of his
    tribe,—
That a ransom might come, and he still might be lost,
And she called to her aid her invention and wit.
She resolved she would steal him, a captive, and flee
To the South, to the mountains; there marry and live
In seclusion, till peace in the nations secure
Made it lawful for them to return to his home.

The Professor.

Daily she sat in her wigwam, contentedly
Drying the venison for future security,
Parching the corn that should serve their necessity;
Fixing her clothing, repairing her moccasins,
Anxiously watching her lover's captivity,
Hopingly, cheerfully doing her drudgery,
Longing for nights with a welcome obscurity,
Rainy and dark, when the moon in its treachery
Could not and would not reveal her complicity;
Watching and waiting, preparing continually,
Hoarding provisions and clothing so carefully.
None ever dreamed that a daughter so dutiful,
Beautiful, kind, could do aught that was mischievous.

   No one had noticed the captive, who wretchedly
Pining in pain, and in dreadful anxiety,
Ever received from this maiden, who lovingly
Bore to his prison, provisions and luxuries;
Aught but a frown, on her features, so stolidly
Gazing at him as a bit of humanity.
Never a smile lit her countenance charmingly;
Never a tear did she shed in his sympathy,
Only a frown on the heart she loved faithfully.

   He had a form that was graceful, majestic,
Heart that was kind, and a face that was beautiful;
He was most noted for daring and bravery;
He was the keenest to watch for an enemy;
He was successful as hunter, or fisherman;

Tradition.

He was the oak, that should shelter her tenderly;
He was the sun, that should light her eternally.

She was a maiden, surpassingly beautiful,
She had a form that was truly voluptuous;
She was ingenious in fashioning moccasins;
She could adorn them with figures quite cunningly;
She could cook food, and could raise it surprisingly;
She was the vine that should bear for him plentiful;
She was the earth, to him gracious and bountiful.

The night was dark the drizzling rain was falling,
The bark canoe was fastened to the shore;
When Nuna, stealing from her father's wigwam,
Began to load the vessel with the corn,
The meat, the clothing, and the stores she'd hoarded,
To aid them in a new, secluded home.

And when in silence all the village lying
Had proved to her that every warrior slept,
She sought the prison of her lover, noiseless,
And clipt the cords that bound his hands and feet,
Then kissed him, whispered " come," and off they started,
And up the Racket flew like frightened deer.

She plied the paddle with a skill consummate,
As silent dipped it, as a fishes fin;
The bright bark sped along, so swift, so quiet,

The Professor.

It seemed as though she'd tamed some monster fish
And harnessed him, to help them on their journey;
Or was, from unseen spirits, having aid.

    His keen eye scanned the shore, his well arm guiding
The little craft, in safety round each turn;
At times assisting in its swift propulsion,
Though long inaction left him wan and weak;
Now love and fear so nerved each weak endeavor,
He still was equal to most common men.

    Just as the morning tinged the east horizon,
They reached a rapid, which they safely passed,
But touched no foot on shore, lest their pursuers,
If any came, should find their trail and then
Continue searching; here in ambush waiting
They quiet lay, and watched the stream till noon.

    As they expected, came a party searching,
Who close inspected every spire of grass,
And every stone protruding from the water,
To find some trace, some speck, or spot, or print
Of feet or bark; the river, kindly rising,
Had washed the stain away, if there was one.

    And when, in long and violent discussion,
It was decided they could not have passed,
They turned the prows of their canoes, and swiftly
Departed for the village with report,

Tradition.

Perchance, to make pursuit in other quarter,
For there were five ways, surely, they could take.

The lovers having been refreshed and rested,
(The one watched while the other sweetly slept,)
Their journey now resumed, and up the river
Continued on, and up, for many days,
Until they reached Long Lake, and on its border
Concluded they would build themselves a home.

The region around was delightful and charming,
The woodland, the marshes, the mountains and valleys,
The lake like a silver sheet stretched to the sunset,
The brook that came chattering down from the hillside
Decided at once where the home should be founded,
And paddling up to a boulder, they landed.

The home they erected was warm and convenient,
Of bark of the spruce tree, though small was substantial,
And chinked with the moss they could gather from boulders,
Well fastened to trees, so that wind could not harm it;
Beside it a spring bubbled up through the pebbles,
That furnished them drink that was cool and abundant.

The hillside was covered with beech trees, and beechnuts

The Professor.

Rained down on the dry leaves whenever the wind blew ;
The hazel that grew by the side of the water,
Gave nuts in profusion ; the lake gave its fishes,
Whenever they hooked them, or speared them by torch light ;
The trout took the hook, and the spear cleft the salmon.

The deer, on the hillside would stare at them daily,
Or wake from their slumbers, graze calm and contented,
'Mid boulders and brakes, or half hid in the bushes,
Would creep to the lake and there browse on the lillies,
As tame as though man was a friend, and a creature
As harmless, as timid, as docile as they were.

One Autumn eve they stood upon a little hill
That overlooked the pleasant vale and lake below.
The mountain side was gorgeous with the varied tints
The frost had put upon the clothing of the trees,
And these, reflected in the bosom of the lake,
That mirrored, also, gaily colored clouds, that hung
In deepest depth of liquid, bluest, purest sky,
That had their painting made by the declining sun.

He long had urged that they should wed, but she, each time

Tradition.

Had always pleaded that the signs were not just right,
And made a hundred weak excuses, such as girls,
And they alone, can make, and always have, and will.
His arm was strong, he urged, and he could bend the bow;
He'd killed a deer that day, and also brought it home;
The paddle he could use, the spear could send with skill;
They should not starve, their store secure; then why not wed?

Upon each side of this fair hill there ran a brook,
That gurgled noisy in the quiet evening air;
These wound and turned amid the mossy trunks of trees,
O'er cobbles, pebbles, gravel, till, uniting, one
Flowed over sand serenely, gently to the lake.
In Spring and Summer flowers bedecked its grassy banks.
And Autumn witnessed ripening fruit, and browning nuts,
But always from the one a quiet music rose.

To his entreaties thus fair Nuna made reply:—
"Go, then, to yonder brook, and bare your feet and limbs,
And walk it downward, o'er the flinty, slippery stones,
And when you meet its fellow from the other side,

The Professor.

You shall find something that shall give you joy for
    life.
Be careful now; slip not, and keep your longing eyes
Full fixed upon the stream; look neither here nor there,
For should you fail much evil may betide. Adieu."

  As she desired he did; he stripped his limbs and feet,
And down the brook as fast as chips would freely float
He waded, stumbling some; his feet were soft, the
    stones
So sharp annoyed him much; at times he almost fell,
But kept his eyes upon the noisy, chilly stream.
And she stole softly to the other brook, and bared
Her ankles brown, and waded down to meet him,
    where
The two were one. She slipped and stumbled, but
    ne'er fell.

  When she approached the spot that she had named
    for him
To find the treasure he so much in heart desired,
She watched his form; it dodged among the trees,
    and she
Then guaged her footsteps to conform in part to his.
When he walked fast, or slow, she longer stepped, or
    short;
Some elbows in the stream deceived her much, at
    times.

Tradition.

He would be going from her, she sometimes from him ;
At length, when he had reached the junction, she was
  there.

An arm round each, a hand in hand, and eyes to eyes,
They walked together down the stream on pebbled
  sand,
Quite to the lake; its little ripples washed their feet ;
There, dipping water with their hands, they bathed
  their brows,
Then each the other bathed, and both the Spirit called
To bless their union sweet with long and fruitful life.
As if in answer to the reverent call, the moon
Rose brightly o'er the mountain top, and sweetly
  smiled.

They dwelt here many years in innocence and peace
With all the world; knew naught of war, and only kept
Their knowledge of their tribes from growing rusty,
  dim,
By visits stealthy made. At times fair Nuna went
Back down the Racket to her old and well loved home ;
She'd manage it to reach there in the night, and stay
Perhaps a month, and sometimes take a little child,
And always came away as slyly as she went.

At times Neota traced the winding Hudson down
Unto its junction with the Mohawk from the west;
And here would visit with his friends of old a week ;

The Professor.

But always leaving when he knew they knew it not.
He sometimes bartered shells, and often brilliant gems
For corn, when his was poor; and he obtained steel
    hooks
From them, and thread to make their clothes, and
    often cloth,   [creased.
So that each year they easier lived, though cares in-

    Children were born in their homes in good time;
Eight noble boys, and six girls at the hearth.
Ruddy and strong were the boys; they could shoot
True to the mark, ere their years numbered five;
Fish they could catch, and the fuel prepare,
Soon as their years counted up half a score;
Quiet they'd creep on the side of the hill,
Searching for deer, and the arrows they sent
Flew to the heart of the buck or the doe,
Straight as the glance from the eye of a maid
Into the soul of the man that she loves;
Surely, by time you could count them sixteen.

    Handsome and kind were the girls; they had eyes
Black as the berries, and bright as a mink's;
Lips that were pink as the shells on the beach;
Teeth that were white as the first flakes of snow;
Voices as sweet as the warble of birds;
Hearts that were kind, and as true as the sun.
Long could they toil with the hoe in the field;

Tradition.

Quick were their fingers in working the beads;
Patient in watching the crows in the trees;
Anxiously tending the couch of the sick,
Cooking the food or in dressing of skins,
Women in knowledge and bloom at sixteen.

When in time, it came round that these parents
Thought a boy or a girl should be married;
Then the mother selected the season,
And she fixed the canoe for a journey
With provisions, and shells for her presents;
And most beautiful stones for the bridal.
Then the youth, much too bashful to venture
In excursion so new, asked the mother
To accompany him down the Racket,
And to give him a fair introduction.
They departed in silence, but always
With a wife, and most joyful, returning.

If a girl was the one to be honored,
Then the father went down the long Hudson
With the fair one, all decked in the gayest
And choicest of ornamentation;
Here he visited friends with his daughter,
Till her eye won the heart of some Mohawk,
And he, yielding his soul to the captor,
In a month, she came back with a husband.
From that time until now we have practiced,
Thus recruiting our tribe from our neighbors;

The Professor.

From the father to son, this tradition
Has been given, and will be repeated.

Chronicle.

As Nicholas concluded his narration,
  My weary friends concluded they 'd retire;
So I'm left " master of the situation,"
  With naught to do but think and keep the fire
Supplied with fuel, as it's growing cool;
And wind my thread of thought upon its spool.

The sage professor 's snoring like a porpoise;
  No doubt he 's dreaming of the hills and valleys,
And reconciling them with the old corpus-
  -cularian philosophy, that tallies
So well with his ideas, no longer mystic;
That fifty years ago were atheistic.

The rest are sweetly sleeping, save the poet;
  He rolls and mutters incoherent words
Of fame and fortune; well he does n't know it;
  When Earth gives fame, it seldom wealth affords;
Be this the motto graven on my stone,
" His highest aim was usefulness" alone.

How beautiful is night, in such seclusion;
  How sweetly silent is the earth and air;
How bright the stars of hope, in such profusion;
  How dark the earth; a soul in blank despair.
Oh, may my heart, with these emotions tender,
Be always charmed with holy, heavenly splendor.

CHAPTER II.

THE TRAVELER.

Chronicle.

The day has not been bright, for frequent showers
 Have broken over us, and damped our ardor;
The brawling brook, with its augmented powers,
 Has robbed us of a portion of our larder.
So that my friends put on their rubber clothing,
To whip the rivers, with a little loathing.

Thank fortune, we have venison yet in plenty,
 And bread, and pork, and other things to match.
Ah! here's the teacher with eighteen or twenty
 As handsome trout as ever man did catch;
And the "Professor" with another dozen,
Which from the stream he has contrived to cozen.

Now then, for supper. "Sam; Cæsar! Nicholas!!
 Here's trout for all; come dress them quick and cook 'em.
To see them eaten will as surely tickle us
 As e'er it did the pedagogue to hook 'em;
He takes delight in taking the poor creatures,
He's such a "taking" way,—like most of teachers."

The Traveler.

The supper's ended and the fish have vanished,
    The guides are bringing order from confusion;
Our gravel floor's repaired and firmly planished,
    Where little puddles stood in great profusion;
The roof is patched, and made a bit more crowning,
So we shall sleep without the fear of drowning.

The clouds have broken, and we see them rolling
    Up, up, along the giddy mountain's side,
All torn and tattered, with the thunder doling,
    Its harshest voices echoing far and wide;
The fleecy folds, like Alpine mountains piling
Above these monsters, seem contemptuous smiling.

'T is twilight hour; the sun's last ray yet lingers
    Upon the cloud that hides the mountain peaks,
And paints them fair, as if an angel's fingers
    Had stole a brush from heaven, and gorgeous streaks
Had spread, with lavish hand upon those domes,
That make us fancy them celestial homes.

The breeze is fresh and cool, and through the spruce
    Is sighing, like a maiden for her lover;
The noisy stream makes not the least excuse,
    But brawls and babbles, rolling round and over
The cobbly bottom, and somewhat annoys us,
As too much of a good thing often cloys us.

Chronicle.

The speaker for the night has had some travel,
  Has gathered shells on many distant strands;
If he should roam in fancy's realm, do n't cavil,
  Accept his gold with the superfluous sands.
These rovers live, you know, by telling stories,—
They rise, and bloom, and fade, like morning glories.

His wampum belt of pictures finely wrought,
  With interwoven shells of modest hues,
From youthful days to later hours are brought
  In great variety, from which to choose.
" From grave to gay," from shallow to sublime,
In sober blank verse, and in lively rhyme.

His life has been as checkered as a map
  That has contrasting colors for each town;
Some large, some small, some square by strange mishap;
A few uncouth in shape; the red, the brown,
The blue, green, yellow, pink and white,
With names in each in letters black as night.

He has a happy faculty in speech,
  That wins a list'ner to his honeyed tongue;
If he in writing, this same point should reach,
  It would be wonderful in one so young.
The winds are hushed, the stars are peeping pale,
So let us listen to the Traveler's tale.

River Shells.

Shells.

The little shells, I found the other day,
    Must serve a text for my twilight discourse;
They bring to mind the scenes of " far away,"
    With all the vividness, and native force
      That first impressed me; now they are the source
From which I 'll draw the finest, fondest dreams.

    These, oft may run in wild and devious course,—
A perfect counterpart, perhaps of streams,
As singing as a shell, that oft with voices teems.
On river banks I've often gathered shells,
    The beach of lakes, and the great ocean's shore;
Admired their beauty, peered into their cells,
    Or listened thoughtful to their mimic roar;
      Have oft compared their species o'er and o'er;
The native and the foreign, with delight
    To find them brothers, by some little score,
Or curious curve, or color gay and bright,
Like youthful hopes, so fair, and yet so frail and light.

Within my native land, Saint Lawrence claims
    From me, from all, the highest meed of praise;
So filled with beauty that the fancy flames,
    And deems those islands poets crowned with bays;
      It moves majestic, silent, sweeps and sways
In graceful curves, or dashed upon the rocks
    That rise resistless in its rugged ways,
And turn the torrent with terrific shocks,
It raves and roars, in wrath, or in derision mocks.

The Traveler.

I 've strolled the banks of fruitful Genesee
    For many miles, bathed in Oswego's wave;
Have viewed the Hudson grand, from source to sea,
    And seen its waters in their beauty lave
The finest scenery nature ever gave
To grace a stream, she gives in all its course,
    From tiny rill, born in the forest grave,
Where dashing cascades bellow harsh and hoarse,
To where it meets the tide with its resistless force.

A hundred others, equally as grand
    In some respects, at home, abroad, have seen;
Crossed some by ferry, some by bridges spanned;
    The Mersey, Severn, and the graceful Seine;
    The Rhone, the Reuss, the Rhine, like serpent green
When seen from Strasburgh's light and slender tower,
    Fed by Helvetia's mountain's icy sheen,
Whose thundering avalanche in midnight hour,
Almost awakes the dead with its tremendous power.

The turbid Thames, with London on each side,
    (The mighty Babylon of modern times;)
Where filth goes reeking, mingling with the tide,
    That seems the fertilizer of all crimes;
    Though church bells ring their ever merry chimes,
Unnumbered heathen dwell within their sound
    In want and wretchedness, and noisome slimes,
Where gaunt disease and misery abound,
And crime of every grade runs in a ceaseless round.

River Shells.

The Tweed, where Scott erected Abbottsford,
   And wrote so charmingly on Scottish themes,
And made all classic ground; in fancy poured
   His brightest jewels in poetic dreams;
   And Bonny Doon, most musical of streams,
To lisp whose name the youngest lassie learns,
   The Highland lover's eye the brighter beams
When on its bank; for as it graceful turns
It sings and sighs a never ending dirge for Burns.

There's scarce a poet ever walked the earth,
   But had some cosy, favorite river's bank,
Where half his glorious visions had their birth;
   Beside, some fount from which he slily drank
   The inspiration of the scene, and shrank
Away from contact with the world; the spells
   He threw around some wild capricious prank,
Were hatched in rivers, and in shady dells— [shells.
They burst, enriched, adorned, and beautified with

On gentle Avon's grassy slope I 've lain,
   Beneath the shade of patriarchal trees,
And dreampt, in fancy, of that loving twain
   Whose names are linked in sweetest memories;
Here had they wandered when the evening breeze
First put the flush upon its tranquil face;
   Learned love from birds, and industry from bees,
Whose sweets, no sweeter than their dear embrace.
They lie beneath one roof. He, noblest of the race.

The Traveler.

I reached this Mecca of poetic hearts,
Will. Shakspeare's tomb, just as the glorious sun
Had gained sufficient light to clear the trees,
And through the stained glass windows flung its light,
In clustered rays of orange, blue and gold,
Upon the slab that hid his sacred dust.
A crown of glory seemed to circle 'round,
And hallow all within and all without;
A sacred stillness filled the atmosphere,
The deep, quick beating of my anxious heart
Almost disturbed the reverential awe
That was pervading all inanimate things.
For once I felt a reverence for a man,
Though dead; and, standing there, seemed lifted up
Into a higher, more etherial air,
And filled with presence of the glorious Past.

His life of toil, of trial and success,
Ran through my mind, a rivulet of facts;
His grand creations that, in my younger days,
I'd seen enacted on the mimic stage,
Came fresh to mind,—a mighty stream, a flood
Of fancied things that overflowed its banks;
Odd scraps of plays, queer anecdotes and songs,
Quotations aptly made and often heard,
Disturbed my brain, like flocks of garrulous birds
'Round rookeries and barns, and all that I
Had ever known of him I knew again.

River Shells.

Here was your mighty dead, (for he still lives),
In silence speaking yet; teaching by precept
Through all coming time, as in time past.
Whose verse, though old is ever fresh and new;
For youth, a source of transport and delight;
For age, a solace for their woes and cares;
For wealth, fine lessons of benevolence;
For beggar struggling with his crust and rags,
A hopeful spirit; and for all, a faith
In universal fitness of great things.

I felt that this was fame, undying fame.
He was not lauded while he walked the earth,
Or hardly known beyond the gray old town;
He had no press to puff with fulsome praise,
His intellectual wares, and few of friends;
He had no clackers in the box or pit
To raise for him vociferous applause;
He never murdered thousands in his time,
Nor reached a throne through seas of human blood;
He made no great discovery in arts,
Nor was a martyr in religious cause;
Science ne'er claimed a votary in him,
And yet his name is cherished in the hearts
Of more true men to-day than any king's
That ever yet has lived, and reigned, and died.

II.

The Traveler.

I 'd stood beside the first Napoleon's tomb
With forehead bared, without a reverent thought;
I 'd been within the crypt of old St. Paul's
Where Wellington and Nelson lie, in peace;
I 'd looked upon Ben. Franklin's modest grave,
And others of our honored, noble dead;
I 'd tramped o'er kings and queens, in Westminster's
Dim aisles, and heard the grand old organ roar,
An avalanche of sound, through sculptured nave
And echoing transept, till the vaulted roof
Trembled in unison with the priestly choir,—
But felt no reverence then, or there, for them.

But here, beside the inanimate dust of him
Who lived three hundred years ago; whose life,
Whose genius lights all modern literature,
And gives a tone to all poetic thought;
Who, seeing little, yet knew all the world,
And more of men and motives that they have
To rule or ruin, more of love and hate,
And those conflicting passions of the heart,
And more of woman than the wisest one
Their sex has yet produced, or ever will;
A new sensation filled my throbbing heart;
In reverence I bowed,—in silent awe.
My youthful hope at length was realized,
And all unconscious of the time or place,

River Shells.

But filled with wealth of happiness, complete,
That welling upward, choking in my throat
At length found vent, in copious, joyful tears.
I searched the Avon's bank and found a shell,
Whose iridescent beauty charmed my eye,
And now while memory or life remains,
It will remind me of that glorious hour.

When I look backward up the stream of time,
  As through a vista of departed years,
Each little transcript of this life of mine,
  A truthful, vivid, photograph appears.
    There fact, instead of fancy, quaintly rears
Again, the scenes I passed in days gone by,   [tears;
    Some crowned with smiles, and others wreathed in
A motly group to any other eye,
On which I cannot look, and then suppress a sigh.

This mountain rill, life's little crystal stream,
  Was born of peaks, and their dissolving snows;
At first a feeble, half remembered dream,
  That flits, and starts, and stops, and scarcely flows;
But winds, and turns, as trembling on it goes,
And gains new power at each successive sweep,
  The ripple skipping, or impetuous throws
Its form and strength in one tumultuous leap,
Adown the ragged front of some wild rocky steep.

The Traveler.

The tiny life-boat of my infant days, [flowers;
That danced, and laughed amid the springtime
With all the joyousness of childrens' plays,
And all the feebleness of childhood's powers;
When life was timid, and the tardy hours
All seemed reluctantly to crawl along;
That brought each day its sunshine, and its showers,
Its pleasures, pains, a never ending throng, [song.
That flashed with life, and light, and jubilant with
Unseen it flows amid the forest glades,
And feebly, faintly, making music rare,
Inhaling incense of the fragrant shades,
That fill, and flush the ever ambient air;
Now sweeps through fields of corn, and meadows fair,
Where busy husbandmen improved the soil,
On past the village, taking on its share
Of labors noble for the sons of toil,
In turning busy wheels, unmindful of the spoil.

I see again, the distant district school,
With pupils crowded, poring o'er their books;
The stern old master and his beechen rule,
Some stand in fear of, or his savage looks;
The girls' play houses, in the fences crooks,
With broken crockery, standing on the rails,
And baby dolls, stowed in their cunning nooks;—
On scenes like this, the memory never pales,
But undescribed still lives, and only language fails.

River Shells.

The boys come rushing from the open door,
   With eager faces and with pattering feet,
Like swarming bees from out the hive they pour,
   Confused and scuffling, to the dirty street.
     To test their strength a couple seem to meet;
Their skill some others, in a game of ball;
   A few, perhaps, contest which is most fleet,
The goal, alas! not towards the teacher's call.
Robust and ruddy, rough and roguish seem they all.

I shut my eyes and think of twenty boys
   Who went to school with me in boyhood's days,
And shared with me my trials and my joys,
   My tasks, perhaps my punishments and plays;
     They're sadly scattered now, in many ways,
With all degrees of varying success;
   A noble few have e'en been crowned with bays;
A part have died, and some have felt distress—
Themselves their greatest curse. Oh, would that they were less.

The brightest, noblest, worthiest of the score,
   Is aided home, a driveling, drunken sot;
My heart, too full of grief to picture more,
   Turns from a theme that only leaves a blot;
     Some ne'er have risen from their humble lot,
And, though the world has moved, are still the same.
   A hopeful few have left the lowly cot,
Ambitious only for a noble name;
And one alone has gained an enviable fame.

The Traveler.

It sweeps among well cultivated farms,
  Through waving grain and cattle-covered hills,
That give the scene one-half its rural charms,
  Its murmuring music eloquently trills,   [fills
    Through nodding groves that line the banks, and
The soul with rapture; through the noisy town
  It crawls, through caverns of the rumbling mills,
That leave its face all ruffled with a frown,   [down.
Or o'er some wild cascade goes flashing, foaming

My life of toil in earnest now begins;
  A clerk for years within the busy mart,
Where brilliant vices tempt the soul to sins,
  And virtue, only, saved the wavering heart,
    That saw the shadows of the deadly smart
Upon the faces of the victims gay,
  And reading as I ran, the easy part
Of their sad lessons, guided night and day
My little bark around the rocks that lined the way.

The many luring islands in the stream,
  Oft tempted me to land my fragile craft,
They promised wealth, these vanished like a dream,
  But hope so buoyant only joked and laughed,
    And, like a debauchee, again I quaffed
The ambrosial nectar; steered for other isles,
  Found those as fruitless; till completely daft
I'm drifting listless, all enchained with wiles
The fates have thrown around me, wreathed in smiles.

River Shells.

On one, I taught a little district school;
    The time was short, thank fortune, aye, or fate.
I should have been much wiser, or more fool,
    And never loitered, but I got my sate,
    And pulled my bark again, at easy rate,
As clerk, or laborer on a splendid farm;
    Then on another did itinerate,
To save the people from the lightning's harm,
But none of these for me, had aught but golden charms.

As engineer on half a dozen more
    I liked to labor, and get its reward;
For gold the wisest often will adore,
    As sometimes Fame neglects her sweet accord,
    And History, heedless, careless to record
Unless gold pays her for her pens and ink,
    With folded hands, sits silent; touch the chord
That gives a silvery sound, and she will wink,
Perhaps will rouse herself, and gaping, try to think.

Upon another, the Historian's task
    I plied with all my vigor, years and years,
Patrolled the country, contracted to ask
    Ten thousand questions of old folks, whose fears
    Were oft excited, and whose eyes and ears
Had lost their cuteness, but whose garrulous tongues
    Would run as easy as the polished gears
Of Waltham watches, and whose healthy lungs
Were strong as working cider, blowing at the bungs.

The Traveler.

And on another little, beauteous isle,
   I drove the pen upon a country journal ;
Do n't deem it fiction, do suppress your smile,
   I really did not find it so infernal
   As many do, whose task severe, diurnal,
Makes them complain ill-natured of their lot ;
   My task, though heavy, was much more supernal,
But wrought with pleasure, there was scarce a blot
Upon my copy ; ah ! I drifted from the spot.
Around these islands, there were dainty shells,
   And shoals, and bars, cascades, and rapids rare,
Where whirling pools sweep round with heavy swells,
   O'er hidden rocks, and boulders black and bare,
   Enticing currents, promised passage fair,
That only led to a tremendous fall ;
   I 've " run the rapids," touching here and there,
And raked my bark, but just escaped the thrall ;
Have lost my little helm, but saved my boat,—that's all.
I try to look ahead ; life's narrow river
   Is shrouded deeply in the mists and gloom,
No cheering ray breaks through with faintest quiver
   The dim uncertainty that hides the tomb.
   Rough rapids yet ; I hear their hollow boom ;
Low sunken rocks, and shoals, and bars of sand,
   With banks well lined with flowers in richest bloom,
That tempt my little boat to touch the strand,
On which I fain would rest, but cannot, dare not land.

Lake Shells.

I 've searched for shells upon the glittering beaches
    Of lakes at home, and some in foreign lands;
Among the pebbles, and long sandy reaches,
    And pressed them lightly in my dallying hands;
    Have gazed with rapture on their brilliant bands,
Their spots, and curves, and mouths, like beauty's cheek,
    Have tossed them in the waves, and seen the sands
Around them nestle, fragile, bright, but weak ;
Like subjects round a queen so modest, mild and meek.

On Skaneateles, brightest of the lakes,
    Where farming lands surround with gentle slope,
And every image that the water takes
    Reflected seems, in grand kaleidoscope.
    The graceful rising hills give vision scope,
The well trimmed hedges, fencing handsome farms,
    The dwellings, barns, and crops, aye all the hopes
Of husbandmen, won by their sturdy arms,
Give life, and light to all of its unusual charms.

On lonely Racket, in the forest dark,
    Where ne'er has rung the ax of pioneer,
But undisturbed, as when the Algonquin's bark
    Its silver ripples cleft, his flashing spear
    Transfixed the salmon, still the timid deer
Can linger, loiter in the coves and bays,
    And feed on lilies, in perpetual fear
Of man, who curiously has learned their ways,
More savage than the native, for he hunts and slays.

II.

The Traveler.

Long, long ago, one evening fair,
    When moon and stars were brightly beaming,
I wandered forth, not heeding where,
    On fortune, fate, and fancy dreaming.
I strolled along the beach of Erie,
    To gather shells beside her wave,
And found beneath a cedar dreary,
    A lone, forgotten, nameless grave.

The grass grew green upon the mound,
    Though seldom washed by Erie's billow;
And, resting 'neath the tree, I found
    It made a soft and easy pillow.
While I reclined, awake, but dreaming
    On such strange thoughts the scenery gave,
A zephyr broke the silence, seeming
    Like whispers from the nameless grave.

" Here lies the dust of one whose aim
    In life, the laurel wreath of glory;
Who sought in every path for fame,
    That he might live in song or story.
Upon life's battle-field contending,
    He toiled, as mad Ambition's slave;
Yet left no deeds with glories blending,
    And found, at last, a nameless grave.

Lake Shells.

"From pity's eye he drew the tear,
  From beauty's breast the sigh of sorrow;
From fervent friends the hearty cheer,
  And lived in hope of fame to-morrow.
He drew a crowd of friends around him,
  And proudly rode the conquering wave;
But lies, alas! where strangers found him,
  And placed him in a nameless grave."

In youthful days I sighed for fame,
  And dreampt of homage paid to writers;
On love for man I based my claim,
  Not hate, like gilt bedizened fighters;
But now, within my bosom swelling,
  These sickening thoughts, attention crave;
Shall some plain mound, of me be telling,
  Here lies one, in a nameless grave?

Shall I, in some neglected spot,
  Without a stake, or stone, to show it,
Or unrespected lie forgot
  By all but those who loved the poet?
Or will some simple song, or sonnet,
  That I have penned, have power to save
My name without a blight upon it,—
  My body from a nameless grave?
    H.

Lake Shells.

The lakes of Switzerland have charmed my eyes,
  A few, not all, in wonder have I scanned;
When Leman's waters woke my glad surprise,
  Beyond I saw Mont Blanc majestic stand.
From bright Brienze, immaculate Jungfrau, grand
  In peerless purity, arose in turn;
  But brightest, sweetest, noblest in that land,
Where patriots' altar fires forever burn,
And light a world oppressed, is lovely Lake Luzerne.

Here Liberty was born, and here baptized;
  Here tyrants learned to fear a people's voice;
Here flew to arms the minions once despised,
  And won their freedom, and proclaimed their choice
  For laws and rulers, with so little noise
It scarce awoke their neighbors,—they who dwelt
  In misery 'round them; other lands rejoice,
And patriot sires their children teach to spell,
And link the brilliant names of Washington and Tell.

The Scottish Lochs have won my warmest praise,—
  Loch Lomond, Loch Katrine, and bright Achray,
Are now the classic ground of ancient days,
  And oft are themes for Scottish minstrel's lay;
  They lie in beauty just as bright to-day,
As when a Malcolm or a Wallace bled;
  The hills as grand, the waves in ceaseless play
Among the shells and pebbles where you tread,
And lovely women still, in Ellen Douglas' stead.

The Traveler.

As I journeyed one morning from lovely Loch Lomon'
  Through the highlands and lakes in a leisurely way,
I espied a most charmingly handsome young woman,
  On her father's bog-meadow patch spreading the hay
As she scattered the locks o'er the newly mown prairie,
  She appeared to my mind much more lovely by far,
Than the brazen, be-diamonded beauties of *Paris*,—
  Though a lusty young lassie of Loch Vennachar.
    A rustic young beauty, a roguish young beauty.
    A ravishing beauty of Loch Vennachar.

Her fair brow had no bonnet to tangle her tresses,
  Which reposed on her shoulders, dark, flowing and free, [dresses,
Decked in one of the shortest and lowest-necked
  That half covered her bosom, and kirtled her knee.
All her movements were queenly, her gestures all graceful;
  I 'd have made her an Empress had I been a Czar.
With a form in perfection, and beauties a face full,
  Was this ringleted rustic of Loch Vennachar.
    A full-bosomed beauty, a brown-shouldered beauty,
    A noble-browed beauty of Loch Vennachar.

She 'd a fine neck and shoulders brunetted and ruddy.
  With twin arms tapered down to her ten finger-tips,
(For all sculptors a model, for painters a study,)
  And a pair of the ripest of ruby-red lips. [healthy.
Dimpled chin moulded strong, cheeks blooming and

Lake Shells.

With her eyes full of mischief, each shone like a star,
And if pearls have a price, she was certainly wealthy,
For a ruddy young beauty of Loch Vennachar,
   A cherry-cheeked beauty, a laugh-loving beauty,
   A starry-eyed beauty, of Loch Vennachar.

Not a stocking or gaiter encumbered her ankles,
  And her feet, finely arched in the instep, were slim,
*(*Ah! a pang of regret in the memory rankles,*)*
  For beside, she displayed a most exquisite limb;
With a waist round and full, justly curved but not slender,
  As the statues of old Grecian goddesses are,
And a smile that, deliciously melting and tender,
  Blossomed over this beauty, of Loch Vennachar.
   A bare-footed beauty, a brown-legged beauty,
   A bewitching young beauty of Loch Vennachar.

Let the Scottish bards sing of their loveliest lasses,
  Or the Troubadours chant of their maids on the Rhine,
Let the Skald of the Dane praise the one that surpasses,
  Or the Savoyard sigh for the girl that's divine,
Let the harpists of Erin praise Limerick ladies,
  Or the Dons for Duenas strike light the guitar;
Let the mandolin murmur for beauties of Cadiz;
  'Tis the pipe wakes the Venus of Loch Vennachar.
   A dazzling beauty, a dallying beauty,
   A dangerous beauty of Loch Vennachar.

The Traveler.

I 've sought for shells upon the Ocean's shore,
    Among the rocks, and in the drifting sand
Along New England's coast found ample store;
    Where Albion's chalky cliffs rose high and grand;
    Where Gaelic tongues, mellifluously bland,
Broke on the ear in sweetest plaintive strain;
    And on the coast of Gaul, that flowery land
Whose beauties charmed without detracting pain,
And language lingers in the mind, a sweet refrain.

A fishing sailor, seeking health to gain,
    I 've dared the dangers of the treacherous sea,
And saw it triumph, like the bloody reign
    Of some old tyrant, sweeping fierce and free
    From off his realm his foes, in highest glee;
I 've seen ingulfed within the yawning wave
    A splendid ship, by tempest's harsh decree,
Without the power a single plank to save,—
A human soul gone down to ignominious grave.

This glorious theme is varied as can be;
    My verse will be as changing as the theme;
'Tis as I found it; it has been to me
    No idle fancy, nor a poet's dream;
    I hope for you to make it truthful seem,
From nature pictured, faithful as the sun;
    And though the flash of fancy oft may gleam,
And brighter tinge the shadows gray and dun,
When gazing at the clouds we choose the brightest one.

Ocean Shells.

Oh, most mysterious, mighty part of earth,
Whose broad expanse extends from pole to pole,
From Afric's sands to Amazonia's flood,
From sunny France and Britain's chalky cliffs,
To where it beats New England's rocky shore;
From ice-bound Greenland to Victoria land;
To thee I raise my feeble song of praise.
   I 've gazed on thee in every varied mood,
From smoothest calm to the overwhelming storm;
I 've seen thee peaceful as a gentle lamb,
And heard thy awful, worse than lion's voice;
By day I 've watched thy changing billows long,
And when the darkness shrouded well thy face,
Have listened to thy surges on the sand.
One phase alone of all thou dost assume
I have not seen; 't is when the hoary king
In stern embrace, locks up thy polar limbs,
And crashing rocks of ice come floating down
To warmer climes to be dissolved once more.
   Let us explore with true Columbian zeal,
The vast foundations of the mighty deep;
And seek among its graceful rising hills,
The vales and plains, the chasms deep and dark,
The intervening mountains, rocks and sands,
The caverns awful, precipices vast,
The plants aquatic, in ten thousand forms,
The groves of coral on the steep hill sides,
The vast shell-covered plain, where beauty lies

The Traveler.

In wondrous shapes, in colors bright and gay,
With graceful curves; the varying volute,
Whose climbing spirals gradually decrease;
The witching bivalves, scolloped fine and true,
Indented, waved, toothed, serrated, or smooth;
Some fine and thin, and white as flakes of snow,
Transparent, almost, as their native brine;
Some quaint, uncouth, with rough and ragged mien,
(Unpolished genius in a rustic garb,)
But beauteous within, like cameos;
The wondrous nautilus, that sinks or sails,
As fear or fancy guides it; hundreds still,
With shapes as various as the varying vales
In which they lie; the orders genus, class,,
Or species proper, of a thousand types,
All flecked or striped with colors blended fine,
To equal which no artist yet succeeds;
The pinkish blush, the sombre, sober brown,
The grassy green, the yellow tint of maize;
The jetty black, with stripes of snowy white
Commingled, adds intensity to both;—
With every shade of hue that forests take
When Boreas breathes a beauty in his blight,
In grand confusion lie amid the bones,
Of stern sea-monsters, or the frames of men,
The grave and gay reclining side by side,
And all united in a charming scene,
A surfeit seems too much to comprehend.

Ocean Shells.

The whales of many tribes; from pole to pole
Their feeding grounds extend; they gave us light;
*(*Othello-like, their occupation's gone.*)*
A hundred other species fit for food,
Must wait for fame from some young Walton's pen.
   A thousand species, seeming useless, roam
At will, and prey on timid neighboring tribes,—
A type of men who live by others faults,
Misfortunes, frailties, vices, fears or crimes.
The pirate shark, voracious, cunning sneak,
A king of robbers, ruthless on the sea;
A foe to all, and each a foe to him,
And many others lower in the class,
Are just beyond my piscatorial lore;
Whose counterparts on land none can mistake,
But claim attention from a Dickens' pen.
   The ocean represents the life of man,
In four short stages, likened to a day;—
When morning dawns, 't is innocence and youth;
When noontide comes, the flush of manhood's prime;
When evening shrouds its face with sombre hue,
A type of toiling, struggling, yielding man;
When night with darkness deadens every sense,
A fitting emblem of the grave and death.
On these I'll dwell, and, in a varied chime,
My facts and fancies weave in changing song,
That in your ears may ring like sounding shells.
II.

The Traveler.

Youth.

Aurora, bright goddess, the Queen of the morning,
    Ascends in the east in her rubicund car,
With golden robes flying, her presence adorning,
    The gem in her forehead a glittering star.
Her fleet-footed coursers now frantic'ly flying,
    On purple clouds leaving their fiery trace;
Now brighter still growing, now fading and dying,
    As Sol o'er the waters presents his bright face.

The waters blue, sparkling, or joyfully dancing,
    As gently approaching they offer a hand,
The white-crested cones much their beauty enhancing,
    Now rising, then falling, now dashed on the strand;
Then slowly subsiding, again are returning,
    Now forward, then backward, are never at rest;
Now sweetly embracing, then tauntingly spurning,
    Till mightier waves their coquettings arrest.

How sweet is their music, how cheerful, how sprightly,
    In quick undulations it strikes on the ear;
Now gently and softly, then touchingly lightly,
    How hopefully pleasant, enchantingly dear;
So soothing, contenting, so calmly consoling,
    And pleading, performing the comforter's part,
So joyf'ly enlivening, and peacef'ly controlling
    The saddened emotions, that rise from the heart.

Ocean Shells.

Now see from her mooring yon shallop departing,
  With crew all aboard and her fleecy sail set;
Like bird for her prey, wheeling, suddenly darting,
  With hearts fondly hoping and blooming cheeks wet
With tears past controlling, from keenest emotion
  At leaving their parents, their birth-place and home,
A venturesome voyage on life's treacherous ocean,
  The highway of nations o'er which they must roam.

How timid it tacks, to the change of the zephyr,
  That dallying toys, like the sirens that sing,
Or bounding away, like the galloping heifer
  When loosed from the stall by the farmer in spring.
Now luffing, contending with breezes blown stronger,
  Or scudding along under double reefed sail;
So gracefully yields what it cannot hold longer,
  Like elms that stand firm, and yet sway with the gale.

Thus man from his infancy seems to be sailing
  The ocean of life, and the journey is short,
With winds of adversity always prevailing
  O'er prosperous breezes, that drive him to port;
The harbor all enter, for none are excepted,—
  The vicious and righteous, the youthful and old;
The good are admitted, the bad are accepted,
  The grave claims us all, with our talents or gold.

The Traveler.

Early Manhood.

In flush of life, when man awakes to glory,
    A frowning rock he stands beside the sea;
With mighty waves around him dashing hoary,
    That ceaseless sing their ill-timed symphony;
Forever telling him the dismal story,
    That warns him often of the stern decree:
That life is labor, labor bringeth life,
Love yields to love, and strife engenders strife.

And thus we liken him unto the ocean,
    When waves are rolling in their majesty,
And sweeping onward, with resistless motion,
    That gains, each bound, impetuosity;
The battle enters, of life's fierce commotion,
    With heart well steeled with animosity;
Each is a foe, and he a foe to all,—
Too weak to conquer, and too brave to fall.

The ocean thus with earth is ever striving,
    And makes his fearful inroads in the sand;
This coast line wasting, on another driving
    The golden grains still higher up the land;
New fields creating, cunningly contriving
    To spread new beauties round on every hand;
And as the land is often changing form,
So men are changed by life's tempestuous storm.

Ocean Shells.

Mind makes the man, and mind is thought immortal;
    The change of ocean lies within the blast;
The mind shall soar and pass its earthly portal,
    A useless relic of a life long past,
To other lands beyond this scene so mortal,
    Where love shall reign forever, first and last;
Old Death forgets not debts due from the living,—
The debt of Life, for which there's no forgiving.

Now slowly rolls the broad, the blue Atlantic,
    The waves unceasing dash upon the shore,
By rough wind borne, and rising so gigantic,
    Make harsher music in their deaf'ning roar;
The sea gulls scream, and sweeping madly, frantic,
    Delighted face the tempest more and more;
Yon lonely vessel slackens quick her sail,
And seems preparing for the coming gale.

The cautious man, in life's tempestuous weather,
    Observes the courses of the floating clouds,
The chart consults, and ascertaining whether
    The ocean currents drift athwart his shrouds,
Examines weeds that float from blooming heather
    To tropic plants, sounds for the shoals, and crowds
Each stitch of canvas, if he fears the coast,
And shuns it as he would a bandit host.

The Traveler.

Manhood's Prime.

The sun behind the western cloud lies hid,
Painting with gold each fleecy pyramid,
With radiant beauty warms, their ever changing forms,
　As they roll in their grandeur on high.
The fresh'ning breezes sing; the flashing spray
Blown from the crests of dashing waves away,
And drifting to and fro, resembles fleecy snow,
　Quite as pure as that bride of the sky;
The awful deaf'ning, roaring, raving blast,
Comes like the plague, stern, terrible and fast.

And man, long struggling with a selfish world,
Sees the bright banner beautifully unfurled;
But mighty storms arise, and hiding from his eyes
　The bright wreath for his brow he would win.
With sails well furled for the opposing blast,
Hope, his sheet anchor, ever holds him fast;
He faces still the breeze, against all toils like these,
　In adversity's clamorous din;
He dares the foe, as vessels dare the billow;
Bends when he must, as yields the weeping willow.

The wind, the waves, in awful concord roar;
Striking in fearful grandeur on the shore.
The quick, the heavy shocks, that beat upon the rocks,
　Make of music the richest and rare.

Ocean Shells.

The hills take up the echo on the land,
Softened by distance, making it more grand.
It sweetly, gently, breaks upon the ear and makes
    It so soothing, there's naught can compare;
    There's nothing sweeter than the "sounding sea,"
E'en fabled Grecian melody, for me.

The vivid lightning flashing from the cloud,
Breaking in awful thunder, quick and loud;
'Tis echoed low and long, with voices harsh and strong,
    And then fainter, now dying away.
    We see the mighty elements at war,
    Fire, wind, and water, and the earth not far,
In battle's grand attire, in fierce and harsh desire,
    To decide which shall conquer the prey.
The ship in flames, the wind, with quickened pace,
Drives her to land, and angry waves embrace.

As calms succeed the storms on ocean's breast,
Mortals desire the days of peace and rest,
And hopeful seek to gain immunity from pain,
    In the hours of their life's sweet decline.
    How few there are, whose hopes were ever high,
    Reap the reward they strive for, e'er they die;
They leave the world in woe, and as they found it, go
    To their graves, at the door of the mine.
The boon they sought was just within their grasp—
Yielding the prize with life's last faintest gasp.
II.

The Traveler.

Old Age.

Age, at night, in drear December,
Trembles on each tottering member,
Clings to life's last lingering ember,
   Whose lone ray is feebly thrown,
For the sighing wind subsiding,
O'er the gentle wavelets gliding,
Drives the snowy crests, while riding
   Each a wavelet of its own;
     Like a mortal riding glories,
       Of the past when hopes had flown,
     To the borders of the ocean,
       There to perish, all unknown.

As each wave each wavelet urges,
And the solemn sounding surges,
Ring their low, unceasing dirges
   For the long lost, loved and lorn;
So we hear the gentle beating
Of a loving heart, entreating
For a short and tearful meeting,
   With the friends we daily mourn;
     For a speedy, heart-felt union
       With the friends beyond life's bourn;
     With the wish that from that meeting,
       We may have a safe return.

Ocean Shells.

Now the waters, growing clearer,
Calmer, making music dearer,
Are reflecting like a mirror
   Fading Luna in the west;
See, the countless stars are glancing
From the waters, and enhancing
Ev'ry beauty, till entrancing
   The poor heart within the breast;
     Till that hoping, fearing, throbbing
     Heart, which needs a day of rest,
     In the fancy, makes these witching
     Stars the mansions of the blessed.

Though thine aged head be hoary,
Man, oh man, where is thy glory?
This last chapter of thy story
   Is so shortly to be told;
As thy steps are graveward tending,
And the ties of friendship rending,
Is thy love of living ending?
   Has thy love of life grown old?
     Has thy life become a burden,
     And too heavy to uphold?
     Has grim death no terror for thee,
     Nor the grave, the damp and cold?

The Traveler.

Old Age.

Hark! the ocean ever sighing,
Makes a sweet and sad replying,
In a language gently dying,
   In the ripples on the land.
" Life is lone, and dark, and dreary,
Of the journey I am weary,"
But the last, the solemn query,
   Was re-echoed mild and bland;
     " Yes," the answer to the question
       Quick was murmured by the strand,
     As the sweet, soft, solemn surges
       Sadly sighed upon the sand.

Chronicle.

The reader ceases as his story ends,
   A lengthened breathing just relieves the quiet;
A somber silence settles on my friends,
   As though their minds had been unsettled by it;
Nor is the stillness of the evening broken
By one unfitly word unthinking spoken.

Chronicle.

The chess-board, empty of its pawns and knights,
   Looks like a little history of the world;
Kings, queens and castles, knocked about in fights,
   That doom the others to oblivion hurled.
All seem to think, (of course I only guess,)
That life, at best, is but a game of chess.

The man who wanders round the beauteous earth,
   And culls no treasure for a leisure hour,
Who cheers no friends, who adds not to their mirth,
   Is quite as useless as a scentless flower.
He may be fair, yes, fine to look upon,
But we expect no music from a swan.

But he who gathers pictures, facts, or shells,
   And makes the world the wiser for his living,
Who notes his journey and his story tells,
   Should have the thanks of men, the women giving
Approving smiles; these compensate him best,
And make a spot feel happy 'neath his vest.

Our lives unto a web are oft compared,
   By fairies woven and with varied dyes,
The joys we've tasted and the pleasures shared,
   The glowing flowers first seen by human eyes;
But underneath in steady, sober gray
The stern realities from day to day.

The Traveler.

How sweetly quiet is the fragrant air,
   How deep the breathing of my sleeping friends,
How softly stars look down, how brightly fair
   The clouds float o'er them, and their beauty ends;
The murmur of the river sinks and swells,
Much like the music of the ocean's shells.

But life to me is like the wampum belt
   By Indians braided with the bark of trees;
The crystal thread of life a breath would melt,
   A tear could snap it or a look could freeze;
Unfelt, unseen, more finely is it spun
Than silk by maids who praise the rising sun.

At first 't is but a little three-strand braid,—
   A silver thread between the rugged twain,
But deftly crossed, with skill close interlaced,
   It twines its crooked course and grows amain,
Till quite a cluster 's added to the band,—
Each child assuming some particular strand.

And on each thread some tiny, pearly shell
   May mark an epoch in a lengthy life,
Some group of beads fantastically tell
   Who won a captive or who fell in strife,
At length is lost, removed by adverse fate,
The only sign, a home made desolate.

CHAPTER III.

THE POET.

Chronicle.

We've had a week of miserable weather,
  So that my friends have scarcely left the camp;
Our roof is soaked, and limber is as leather,
  And leaks so badly everything is damp.
My wits, alas! have had a thorough soaking,
And all unfitted are for much dry joking.

The leaves are weeping, ev'ry thing is dripping;
  Pools, puddles, ponds, with rivulets and rills,
Surround the camp, and from it we've been dipping
  The dirty water which each hollow fills.
Tis water, water everywhere, we think,—
Not good enough for temperance men to drink.

I've watched the rain drops trickle from the spruces,
  And seen the little pools beneath the branches
Increase each moment, then the brooks, like sluices,
  Flow to the river, as a youth that launches
Into the stream of life his little shallop,
Which rushes onward at a fearful gallop.

The Poet.

The little rivers have for days been rushing
    With swollen tides, impetuous and roiled;
One night some driftwood coming down went crushing
    Our fragile bridges, so that they are spoiled.
The little rill that trickled down the mountain,
Became a brook and overflowed our fountain.

There's not a fern leaf bowing with its load
    Of diamond drops upon its feathery fringe,
But gives a fragrance; stumps are the abode
    Of sweetest odors; logs, decaying, tinge
The air ambrosial with their nectarine essence,
That seems oppressive in its copious presence.

How beautiful, how varied are the mosses
    That cling to rocks, and earth, and logs and trees;
The sweetest flower the sunny south wind tosses
    With wanton breath, is no more bright than these:
So fair, so fine, so fresh, so frail, so tender,
Like woman's love, in all things sweet—and slender.

Some species grow in such exuberant masses,
    That they seem forests in quaint miniature;
Each little sprig a tree is; other classes
    Resemble vines, and cling to trees secure.
Among the rocks there often can be seen,
A velvet couch well worthy of a queen.

Chronicle.

The camp-fire burns, but not with usual brightness,
   The wood is damp, and smoke comes in our faces;
Our hopeful hearts have lost a little lightness,
   And fretful feelings fill those pleasant places.
Avaunt, ye doleful thoughts! the wind is shifting,
The rain has ceased, the heavy clouds are lifting.

All things are glorious! In the south and west
   A yellow strip between the mountain bases
Proclaims the ending storm; the dripping vest
   Of nature, flapped by breezes, gives our faces
A happier glow; there'll be no more restrainment
Upon our usual twilight entertainment.

The week has passed most wearily with all
   Except the youth, Poeta; he has written
Such scores of verses; coming at his call
   Seemed every Muse, with the young genius smitten.
If ever poet needed aid divine,
He should have had it from the tuneful nine.

We tell him he is moony; that the glowing
   Sensation, thrilling, dancing in his nerves,
Could all be hushed, if he would practice rowing
   Or other exercise; it often serves
To cure a case of chronic indigestion.
That this is all that ails him there's no question.
   III.

The Poet.

His flowing locks, luxuriant on his shoulders,
   In wavy masses hang, like country maiden,
Brown as the moss in summer on the boulders
   That line the forest, and with glories laden.
His Byron collar folded o'er his coat,
And fastened with a ribbon at the throat.

He may be twenty, looks like seventeen,
   The beard has scarcely started on his cheeks,
Which show some freckles; he's a bashful mien
   That makes him look much younger; when he speaks
His girlish voice so tremulously trills,
The heart melodeous with its music fills.

His face has not a line of beauty beaming,
   As oft we notice in poetic pictures;
No "flashing eye," no "radiant brow," and "seeming
   A citadel of thought," (excuse my strictures);
Of course you'd like to know just how he looks,—
The picture's truthful as the best of books.

'T is twilight hour; again we all assemble,
   To hear the youth in dulcet strain rehearse
His latest labor; the delicious tremble
   That gives a charm peculiar to his verse,
Will join the whisper of the evening breeze,
That tilts the leaves of the deciduous trees.

The Dream.

The camp-fire's bright, the glowing warmth is pleas-
 ing,
The feeble crackle of the licking flames,
The sparks ascending, and the breezes teazing,
 The sighing spruces, each attention claims;
But sights, or sounds, all others now unheeding,
Save one,—we'll listen to the poet's reading.

The Dream.

Last week I wandered from the haunts of men,
And sought a wild and most romantic glen;
I traced a river's course unto its smallest source,
 And the grandest of fountains had found;
I felt the virgin forest's odorous air,
With fragrance laden of the flowers rare,
The aroma was shed, by e'en dying and dead,
 As they spread their crisp leaves o'er the ground.

Above me rose, majestic in the west,
A towering cliff in gorgeous colors dressed;
I trembling stood and gazed, like one that's half
 amazed,
 To behold this magnificent scene.
A thousand feet, and more, above me rose
The wall gigantic, and in calm repose,
At its foot mighty rocks, that the earth in its shocks
 Had hurled down from its forehead serene.

The Poet.

The stinted spruces on its lofty brow,
Like grizzled hair, in straggling locks, endow
Each crag, and point, and seam, until they fairly
    gleam
    With intelligence, old as the world;
  The perpendicular places seemed to be
  The tablets, where old Time had written free,
In the days of the past, that were chiseled to last,
    Till the earth into chaos is hurled.

  The mighty fallen masses at its base,
  That Nature tore convulsive from its face,
In wild confusion lay, in ev'ry form and way
    That the mind can in fancy conceive;
  The bushes, trees, and shrubs of various kinds
  Grew lovingly among them, and the winds,
So delightfully still, that the ring of the rill,
    In its laughter compelled me to grieve.

  Aquilla perched upon a jutting shelf,
  And stretched his pinions, ere he poised himself
To sail majestic through the vast etherial blue,
    He surveyed his imperial throne;
  A scream he uttered, terrible and wild
  As mothers give who see a drowning child,
Then exultingly springs, as he spreads his broad
    wings,
    O'er the land that's entitled his own.

The Dream.

The crystal stream that murmured at its foot,
Refreshing, feeding ev'ry fibrous root,
The sweetest music made, beneath the grateful shade,
    As it ran in smooth ripples along;
Above the eagle had her noble nest,
And forest song-birds had a place of rest;
While the voice of the thrush did in melody gush
    Through the grove, as she sang her sweet song.

I liked to linger in this lovely spot,
And leave the world, with all its crimes, forgot,
And did; until the sun, through smoky mists looked
    dun,
And the light had grown dim on the plain;
I then reclined upon a mossy mass,
And thought I saw dim-visaged specters pass;
For the blue dusky light half bewildered my sight,
    And my mind was in fanciful train.

The dreamy mists were gathering on the scene,
In wavy clouds, with rays of light between,
And as they slowly rolled, with edge of crimsoned
    gold,
That reflected the rays of the sun,
They were resolved in many varied forms
Of fancy shapes, or tumbled as by storms,
Like the waves of the sea in their boisterous glee,
    As in quaintest of by-ways they run.

The Poet.

The somber clouds were hovering round me,
   Half veiling plain and stream, yet I could see
Aquilla slowly come back to his airy home,
   As he circled around his mate's nest;
Behind him followed an enchanting train,
   Sweet music making a celestial strain ;
Oft their notes would prolong on the words of the song,
   And my ear, until now, was ne'er blest.

Apollo struck his ever tuneful lyre,
   In perfect concord with his vocal choir;
Minerva smiling stood, in noblest attitude,
   And surveyed the fair region around ;
She waved a hand that bade each echo cease;
   There stood the gods and goddesses of Greece,
As they often of yore had assembled before;
   I observed them in silence profound.

Upon a gorgeous stage they seemed to stand,
   In several groups, round chiefs who gave command,
In flowing garments dressed, whose foreheads high were pressed,
   By the crowns that proclaimed them the kings,
In modest vesture was each female form,
   With radiant faces, smiling, sweet and warm ;
And the gems that they wore from the Lethean shore
   Were obtained ; neither bracelets nor rings.

The Dream—Minerva.

Aquilla, perched above the gorgeous throng,
Attentive listened, till they closed the song;
Then uttered one low note, through rough and savage
    throat,
  Thus his message to me did he break,
"Oh, mortal!" said he, or he seemed to say,
"Minerva teaches, list to her I pray."
Then as soft as the wind, as it sighs through the lind,
  Thus the Goddess of Wisdom then spake.

———

Much envied mortal, favored of the gods,
For those like thee we leave our grand abodes.
Aquilla summoned, we obeyed his voice
To give thee aid, and much approve his choice;
Attend thee then, drink deeply of the store
That we provide, more rare than human lore,
For erring men, who long have taught you youth,
Still grope in blindness, seeking for the truth.
  We long have watched with hope thy rustic cot:
With pleasure viewed thy honest, humble lot;
And though the dear-bought brazen trumpet fame,
Has never echoed with thy modest name;
Though brother bards have never sung thy praise,
Nor gentle woman crowned thy brow with bays;
Still thou art blest, and not without a cause,
For earth will yet resound with thy applause.
  III.

The Poet.

We have loved bards with whom we were content,
Whose lives, approved by us, were chiefly spent
In praise of Nature, or her handmaid, Art,
With not an o'erdone or a stinted part;
With little reverence for the thoughts of men,
Whose shriveled minds despised the plow-boy's pen.
To such a one, my mind instinctive turns,
The loved, regretted, envied poet,—Burns.
    Frail bud of earth, the task to thee assigned,
Will be to picture nature to mankind;
To aid thy fellows in the road to right;
To peace, and love, and liberty, give light;
To strike oppression with a deadly blow,
And give to charity a brighter glow;
To spread the truth with ever willing hand,
With all the strength that mortals can command.
    But seek no praise for doing what is right,
And aid the needy, struggling in the fight;
The strong have ever yet the weak oppressed,
But then the wealthy are not always blessed.
    Seek not for fame, 't is vanity in men,
It comes unsought to those who wield the pen,
Be patient, labor; merit wins renown,
But toil and genius claim the laurel crown.
We know thy mind is fraught with passion strong,
Which often bursts in wild enraptured song.
But guide it close, within the truthful course,

The Dream.—Poet's Fate.

And let it swell with all its native force ;
Give scope to fancy if thy end 't will gain,
But guide it truly with a steady rein ;
Fear not the scoffs of those who would be wise ;
Have our approval, and let that suffice.
    We urge thee then, to grasp the poet's pen,
And let thy thoughts run riot among men ;
Write for the largest liberty defined ;
Write for the noblest liberty, the mind ;
Write for the dearest liberty, the press ;
God's all-approving will applaud and bless.
We know the woes around thee will be great,
But be prepared, this is the poet's fate.

When first the youth takes up the poet's pen,
    He sees all Nature through his fancy's prism,
And views new fields, unknown to other men,
    And thus attracts the shaft of criticism,
    Or filthy taunts of petty plagiarism ;
Although his aim be holy as Saint Paul's,
    He is arraigned and charged with skepticism,
By which at once his fine-built fabric falls.
He firmly meets his fate, and naught his heart appals.
    III.

The Poet.

He heeds not scoffs, or taunts of petty foes,
    Nor takes advice of firm and trusting friends,
But battling well betwixt conflicting blows,
    The odds unminding, bravely on contends;
    By nobler means obtains his wished-for ends,
Well pleased at heart at his dear-bought success,
    Pursues his rugged way, nor even bends
His course, to seek well-merited redress;
But pays them all in time, with interest, ne'ertheless.

Then woman brings a trouble in his heart,
    And through his heart she steals away his brains;
She knows by instinct they can never part,
    For love electric-like forever reigns
    In woman's breast, and if she takes the pains,
She sends a shock that will subdue at will
    The man she sighs for, managing the reins
With care, in hopes to draw him tighter still;
So like the feline race, she captivates to kill.

Some witching female, budding into bloom,
    Appears before his much bewildered mind,
And nightly dreams predict his final doom,
    Though minds are changing as an April wind;
'T is love that makes all men and women blind
As ever Homer was in days of yore;
    Till disappointment opes their eyes, they find
A wholesome truth they could not know before,—
That they are mortals all, alas! and nothing more.

The Dream—Poet's Fate.

He seeks the columns of a noted paper,
   In which to lay his thoughts before mankind,
And sees afar his fancied prospects vapor,
   As flies the mist before a morning wind;
For critics scan the faults they think they find,
And magnify the errors of the pen;
   Though genius flashes brightly, they are blind,
Believing poets only common men;
As if true genius were within the critic's ken.

But nothing daunted at the ill success
   With which he seems to meet the critic's taste,
He tries a theme of which they know still less,
   And has the fate to be condemned in haste;
   Although in language beautiful and chaste,
In thought and diction forcible and strong,
   Conceiving it to be a useless waste
Of time and talent, to convince them wrong,
He leaves them to their fate, poor judges of a song.

But often times a heart within the land,
   That beats responsive to the poet's strain,
Is swayed, as when the ocean wild and grand
   Is dashed on rocks that check the raging main,
   Or when through forests, joining its refrain,
The blast is singing, or a mother's prayer
   Like breezes dallying with the waving grain;
It garners up the treasures rich and rare,
From which to cull, some day, a chaplet for its fair.

The Poet.

'T would take a month to tell one-half the woes
    That cluster round a poet while he sings;
How friends abuse him or become his foes,
    And hope deferred, pale melancholy brings;
    How fortune flies on ever fickle wings,
How grim disease annoys a dreaded guest;
    How poverty's cold pang; the bitter stings
Of hunger, that imploringly infest
The hovel of a man who always should be blest.

He drags a weary wretched life along
    A few short years, that seem almost an age,
While busy hopes and fancies round him throng,
    And care for fame has made him quite a sage;
    His name unknown upon historic page;
His useful life all seeming thrown away;
    He makes his exit from the author's stage,
And droops from notice in the public way;
In hopes of this reward, "To Memory," some day.

Compelled by age, he seeks an humble shed,
    In which to pass his last, neglected days;
Unpillowed lies his fevered throbbing head,
    His aching limbs convulsed are tossed all ways;
    To Nature's God serenely, calmly prays,
That for all sins he may in peace atone;
    On him Hope sheds her most benignant rays;
Though o'er him genius had its mantle thrown,
Alone he dies, "unknelled, uncoffined and unknown."

The Dream—Minerva.

A few, perhaps, may recollect his name,
   And fewer still are those who quote his verse;
No pen is lifted to award him fame,
   Or with faint praise to do a deed far worse;
   Some antiquated book-worm, like a nurse
In after years, a resurrection brings;
   Some grand interpreter can then rehearse
The lines that live; the thought that fairly rings,
And gives a joy to those whose intellects are kings.

At length the grass grows o'er him fifty years,
   Then anxious pilgrims from a dozen climes
Will seek his grave, bedewing with their tears
   The turf that covers this poor man of rhymes;
   His virtues then by far outweigh his crimes;
   His heart long perished cannot harbor guile;
   His name alive, though dead in his own time,
Resounds with fame to earth's remotest isle,
And stranger hands erect the monumental pile.

   Minerva ceased, the sweetest breezes sighed,
   And gentle echo dying then replied;
The choir celestial sung, the harp enchanting rung,
     With the grandest of music around.
   Calliopy advancing full of grace,
   With love and beauty beaming in her face,
Joined her voice, sweet and strong, in the words of the song,
     Till the harp and the choir all were drowned.
III.

The Poet.

Advancing, then, Æolus took the stand;
He seemed like one well fitted to command,
His voice rang soft and free, sonorous as the sea,
    When a storm in a calm dies away;
His manner noble. grave and dignified,
    As conscious of his worth, not puffed with pride;
And the crown that he wore, was enriched with a store
    Of the flowers that flourish in May.

Thus he began :—Frail youth attend a while,
And let my words thy simple mind beguile.
Sing when thou canst and ne'er with pride refuse
The proffered aid of e'en the humblest muse.
And if for music thou wouldst write thy song,
As soft as zephyrs let it flow along.
If in stern language thou thy wrath wouldst pour,
Then let it roll, a grand tornado's roar.
These two extremes, the compass of my voice,
Give range enough from which to take thy choice.
The four great winds in elemental strife,
Are emblematical of human life :—
A four-stringed harp on which a thousand airs
Are played with ease, of hopes, and joys, and cares.
All poets present, and all poets past,
Have praised their music, and an army vast
Of authors, scribblers, rhymers, always find
A soothing consolation in the wind.

The Dream—Æolus.

The penny whistle in the school-boy's lips,
Is wind, but music, to the girl who skips;
The lover's sigh unto the self-same maid,
Is music still, by answering sigh betrayed;
The soldier's charge upon the sanguined plain,
Is music still; she listens and again
The last kind word, the latest lingering breath,
Is music to her till 't is hushed in death.
Advance, ye muses! Join the vocal ring,
And aid the winds in their attempt to sing.

The crowd advanced, again approving smiled;
Apollo, who with music rare and wild,
With all the gifts of art, such sweetness did impart,
    That the mountain re-echoed the strain;
The melody rushed river-like along,
The muses, nymphs, and naiads joined the song,
And the spruce-scented breeze that just rustled the
    trees,
    Spread the sound, rich and rare, o'er the plain.
III.

The Poet.

The Winds.

Hear the eastern, morning wind,—
    Vernal wind, balmy wind;
Fresher, purer, dearer, sweeter, clearer,
    Than the voice of Lind.
Now it brings refreshing showers,
Singing birds and fragrant flowers;
    They are springing, incense flinging,
    Hear them singing, pleasure bringing,
    Hill, and dale, and groves are ringing
        With their songs.
    Now the breezes softer sighing,
    And the little birds replying,—
    In the distance echo dying,
        Still prolongs.
Now in balmy zephyrs blowing
O'er the flowers so frailly growing,
        Hear it gush,
As it kisses pinks and posies,
And embraces all the roses,
        See them blush.
As it gathers their perfume
From the petals and the plume,
        How it sighs;
Now it wafts it o'er the fields,
And its dearest incense yields
        As it dies.
Making piteous appeals
        With its cries

The Dream—Winds.

Now it flies,
        And it sighs,
                As it dies;
Faintest echo still replies.
      Hark again, 't is growing stronger,
      And 't is sweeter, lasting longer,
For the clouds now like a pall,
That are hanging over all,
        Bring the brightest, warmest showers,
        To refresh the drooping flowers;
Earth is blooming, fresher, fairer,
Shedding incense sweeter, rarer;
        Little warblers of the grove,
        Sweeter sing their songs of love;
And the music that they make,
On the senses seems to break
                With a glow;
Such as angels sing forever,
And poor mortals sigh for, ever
                Here below.
Youthful hopes, and youthful pleasures,
Youthful sports, and youthful treasures,
        Free from every care and sorrow,
        Looking anxious for the morrow,
              Day by day.
Hear their laughing merry shout,
Ringing gaily, gladly out,
              In their play.

The Poet.

Hear the Southern mid-day wind,
      Summer wind, gushing wind;
Blowing stronger, wilder, fuller, fresher,
      From the isles of Ind'.
Now the spicy breeze is coming,
And the busy bees are humming;
      They have found us, buzzing 'round us,
      They surround us, and have bound us,
      For their little wings confound us
           With their din;
      Now they're off to gather honey,
      While the atmosphere is sunny;
      Like a miser seeking money,
           They must win.
Now in fresher breezes blowing,
Halting, stopping, gushing, going,
           Sweeping by;
How it sways the fields of clover,
And in wavy ridges over,
           See it lie.
Now its fragrant essence shedding,
Which the wanton breeze is spreading,
           How it mourns,
Wooing flowers it finds its blunder,
Beauty torn from youth asunder
           Ne'er returns,
Hope that stands aghast with wonder,
           Only burns.

The Dream—Winds.

Hearts that yearn,
Often learn,
They must spurn,
When for love there's no return.
Now 'tis growing mild and warm,
And foretells a thunder storm;
For the clouds are black as coal,
And the distant thunders roll;
See the vivid lightning flashing,
Hear the darkened forest crashing,
Birds are flying, hiding, screaming,
Frightened by the terror seeming,
Till the storm is fairly over,
And the flattened fields of clover,
Raise their heads that have been drooping;
And the birds, that have been grouping
In the trees,
With their plumes in ruffled sadness,
Shout aloud their notes of gladness
To the breeze.
Loving hearts, in loving kindness,
Loving eyes, in loving blindness,
Full of hope and aspiration,
For a nobler situation,
Far above,
Hear him pledge his hand and heart,
Until death alone shall part
Them in love.

The Poet.

Hear the Western, evening wind,
   Autumn wind, chilling wind;
Whistling longer, stronger, ruder, wilder,
   Through the yellow lind.
Now the trees, with rainbows dyeing,
Shelter birds that southward flying;
   At their leaving, sorely grieving,
   So bereaving, no retrieving,
   Fondly hoping and believing
     Once again,
   That when flowers are freshly springing,
   Songs of love they will be singing,
   Till their joyous notes are ringing
     O'er the plain.
Now the blast is stronger, colder,
Woods are looking grim and older,
     And they roar;
Withered leaves are rustling, flitting,
Which the screech owl, most befitting
     Might deplore.
Hark! the branches writhing, bending,
Creaking, moaning, groaning, blending
     With the blast;
Snapping, crashing, they are falling,
With a dismal sound appalling.
     Thick and fast,
As though fiends aloud were calling
     On the past.

The Dream—Winds.

Hear the blast,
      Rushing past,
           Fierce and fast,
And the sky is overcast;
    Now 't is growing rough and loud,
    Rolling on the inky cloud,
Harsh and fiercer, in its groaning,
Is the forest louder moaning,
      Deeper, lower, is the roaring,
      Of the rain in torrents pouring,
Spreading gloom around the fountain,
'Mong the flowers that decked the mountain;
      Gloomy death in peace reposes,
      On a couch of withered roses,
Making Nature look so sober,
When the days of sweet October
           Pass away;
That the winds in grief are sighing,
And the forests are replying
           To their lay.
Manhood's toils, and manhood's trials,
Manhood's struggles and denials,
      Firm of purpose, full of daring,
      Pushing onward, nothing sparing,
           For the spoil;
Winning wealth, or fame, or glory,
On the golden field, or gory,
           See him toil.

The Poet.

Hear the Northern, midnight wind,
   Winter wind, blasting wind;
Sounding rougher, harsher, fiercer, coarser,
   Till the ear is dinned.
Hark! the rapid rushing river,
Roaring, raving, makes us shiver,
   Hear it dashing, tearing, splashing,
   Trees are clashing, ice is smashing,
   And the mountain torrent crashing
     With a roar.
   Night is slowly darker growing,
   Ghastly gloom on all bestowing,
   And grim desolation sowing
     Roughly o'er.
Now the gale is fiercer, bolder,
And 't is growing keener, colder,
     And the sound
Deadly dismal is, and howling,
As a famished wolf that's prowling
     Fiercely round.
Now in mournful cadence moaning,
'Mong the trees in direful groaning,
     On it goes;
Faster, fiercer, wilder, rougher,
Stronger, colder, harsher, tougher,
     Still it blows;
Darker, drearer, blacker, bluffer,
     Full of woes.

The Dream—Winds.

Now it blows,
   And it snows ;
     As it goes
All the icy rivers close.
  Crystal flakes are faster drifting,
  Higher, harder, they are lifting ;
Hill and dale and mountain moor,
They are wafted swiftly o'er,
  And the blighting chilling gale,
  Rushing through the lonely vale,
Brings a terror to the dwelling,
As around 't is harsher swelling ;
  For the trees are snap'd asunder,
  With a noise like cracking thunder,
Sweeping harmless through the willow,
Rolling high the foaming billow
     With its breath ;
Making earth sad, dark, and lonely,
Fit for demons, and those only
     Who love death.
Age of pain, and age of weakness,
Age subdued to faith and meekness,
  Totters on toward the ferry,
  Where old Charon, with his wherry
     On the wave,
Takes the trav'ler, weary, willing,
For his last, long-hoarded shilling
     To the grave.

The Poet.

The tones celestial filled my anxious mind
With thoughts enchanting, glorious, refined;
And as the music grew melodious and new,
    The great mountain the echo prolongs;
The vocal choir their sweeter voices raise,
With words harmonious as an angel's praise;
But the meaning they bore on the Stygian shore,
    Was much more than to mortals belongs.

Advancing grand the chief of chiefs then came,
Whose eyes were brilliant as a diamonds flame;
His hair in masses hung, and o'er his shoulders flung
    A gray beard, like Elisha of old;
The massive crown above his forehead bare,
Composed of pearls, and rich with rubies rare;
And the voice of their king had a crystalline ring,
    As he read from his parchment unrolled.

Oh, forest bard, attend! To thee I bring
    A proclamation unto all who write,
But more especially to those who sing,
    And dear assistance of a muse invite:
The sun is breaking through the gloomy night
That like a cincture thralled the minds of men;
    The Press has power uncounted; used aright,
A force Archimedean; it is then
But guided and controlled by those who wield the Pen.

The Dream—Jupiter's Proclamation.

Oh! come, as waves come rolling to the shore;
   Oh! come, like rivers rushing to the sea,
And come resolved, henceforth and evermore
   To aid mankind till ev'ry one is free
   To sit unharmed beneath his vine and tree;
The product of his labors to enjoy;
   Like brethren live, fulfilling the decree;
Then, all in peace and love, none will annoy,
And earth will then rejoice with great exceeding joy.
The world is calling loudly for reform,
   And you, the poets, must obey the call;
So ev'ry one who feels his heart grow warm
   With love of freedom, must help roll the ball,
   Till tyrant kings and petty despots fall.
Man was not born to live and die a beast;
   No! nobler far was the design for all;
Nor be a slave to king, pope, prince or priest,
Nor filthy weeds, in fact, nor rum to say the least.

First, land monopoly, earth's greatest curse,
   The cause of want, war, slavery and woe,
That makes good, bad, and makes the bad still worse;
   Shall it permitted be? Shall it be so?
   I think I hear an echo answer, "No!
The time shall come when equal rights shall reign;
   When brother shall not deem his brother low,
Nor poverty be seen with deep disdain,
But blessings crown us all alike, as nature's rain."
   III.

The Poet.

Next, monstrous war; the victims of its rage,
    Unnumbered millions, loudly sue for peace;
It seems as though, in this enlightened age,
    That bloody wars and butcheries should cease;
    That love for man should be on the increase,
As was foretold in ages long ago;
    Will man enlightened ever bring release,
From murder, rapine, misery and woe?
He has not done so yet, and never may; none know.

Five thousand years have rolled their ceaseless course,
    Still millions of old Noah's sons are slaves,
In doomed disgrace, to toil by Canaan's curse,
    And millions more have found their narrow graves,
    O'er which the grass luxuriantly waves;
Though not a stone tells where the martyrs lie,
    Whose lives were sacrificed to selfish knaves;
Afar from lands that own them still, they die,
On civilization's page, a blot of deepest dye.

The world, long ruled by Emperors and Kings,
    Who claimed to govern by a right divine,
Their subjects treated as the vilest things
    That crawl the earth beneath their reptile line;
    In mind imbecile, and in strength supine,
No question rose among them of the right;
    Until ambitious people could combine
To rid the world of their unholy blight;
Then all in freedom's name, though right or wrong,
    would fight.   III.

The Dream—Jupiter's Proclamation.

Oh, black licentiousness! the worst of crimes
    That.'s been enacted by your mighty ones,
By those it seems, "as hell possessed" sometimes,
    By more than mortal, more than earthly sons;
Since Adam's time the mighty torrent runs,
    And fiercer, stronger, still it sweeps along,
The dangers thicken, and the bark that shuns
The giddy whirlpool, or the channel wrong,
Is more than mortal man, and does not here belong.

The fiend intemperance has raved on earth
    As long as you have records of the past;
Like other monsters, it was weak at birth,
    But now 't is growing overwhelming fast;
Its power mighty and its influence vast,
    'T is sweeping millions to the drunkard's grave,
Where all who drink the poisons stop at last,
And only those who battle fiercely, brave,   [wave.
The tempest can withstand that rolls the conquering

A mighty host, they of the Blackstone school,
    Need much reform, aye, more than I dare name;
They sell their talents, and become the tool
    Of clique or party; bring disgrace and shame
    On their profession; injure their fair fame,
Till half their clients wish they were in hell,
    Where lives their father, so 't is said, in flame;
But where I trust, no mortal yet did dwell,
And, as it 's after death, I know not, none can tell.

The Poet.

The worthy followers of Galen's art
  Make much ado about some sovereign pill,
As though their trade is wounded to the heart,
  By some poor quack, whose ignorance, not skill,
  One panacea has for every ill;
If they would use the talents they possess,
  To seek for truth, and not a lengthy bill,
Mankind would suffer from diseases less,   [bless.
And now, where thousands curse, a million sure would

The ministerial guides from earth to heaven,
  Now, as of old, are guilty of foul crimes;
The love of women, wine and gold has driven
  To rashness many, some to foreign climes;
  It seems as though in these enlightened times,
That they should practice strictly what they preach,-
  Should work for man, and not for paltry dimes;
Be doing good to all within their reach,   [teach.
And let fair science rule the thing that they would

If ignorance is the mother of all crimes,
  Should not the youth be educated free?
Should wealth untold be sent to foreign climes
  To aid the heathen, when you daily see
  The heathen here, where they ought not to be?
Should ye in ignorance let your children die
  The death of felons, robbers; thieves, and ye
Be held not guilty of a deeper dye?   [lie.
On those who frame the laws, the darker crime shall

The Dream—Jupiter's Proclamation.

You who have power to wield a Byron's pen
  On nobler themes, should now employ your prime
Than love-sick dreams at murmuring streams, for then
  Your thoughts, ennobled in heroic rhyme,
Should both be read and felt in your own time,
  Not left to mould till you are with the dead;
Go write for freedom, heartfelt, yet sublime,
  And o'er the world a happy influence shed, [bled.
And you may win a name as though you 'd fought and

Uphold the doctrine that all men are free,
  That all are equal, black and white the same;
Have rulers made by men, not heaven's decree,
  By men removed, too, if they are to blame;
And banish slavery—every type 's a shame;
  Wealth should not govern; equal rights to all,
Climes, colors, nations, sexes, race and name;
The bond of friendship binding great and small,
And one grand chain of love surround this earthly ball.

And advocate man's right to own the soil,
  And universal everlasting peace;
That none should live by unrewarded toil;
  The reign of Kings and Emperors should cease,
  And non-producers be on the decrease;
And base licentiousness should be unknown,
  And gross intemperance would find release
With want and woe, when misery had flown,
And happiness would reign, a blessing now unknown.

III.

The Poet.

The murderer should not raise the fatal knife,
   And vile intolerance should not show its face;
The lawyers have no cause for mental strife,
   Physicians be a blessing to the race,
   And education take exalted place;
Religion should not be a gaudy show; |brace.
   Pure thoughts and words each author should em-
And smooth the path for wretched man to go
To an eternal life, while fitting here below.

Oh! come, as waves come, innocent yet strong;
   Oh! come, like winds, heard, felt, and yet unseen;
And as the light of heaven rolls along,
   O'er barren mountain tops and valleys green,
   Give light to all; let nothing intervene;
Love all mankind, and use your efforts, too,
   To free them all, body and mind, and mean
To do to others as you'd have them do,
Under like circumstances, always unto you.

Apollo left his most melodious lyre,
   As Jupiter retired behind the choir,
Then with majestic stride, with Venus by his side,
   He advanced to the front of the host;
   He filled a goblet seemingly with wine;
No juice of vine, whose tendrils intertwine
'Round a rock or a tree, all so loving and free,
   But of nectar he drank off his toast.

The Dream—Apollo.

Oh! mortal! Thou long envied of my train,
With heartfelt hopes I now this goblet drain;
Thy life, thy health, thy happiness and fame;
Thy hopes, success, thy prospects and thy aim,
Are dear to me, to all who hear me now,
For all admire the poet of the plow.
    Oft have we heard in our celestial sphere,
Thy voice melodious, filled with hope and fear,
Thy plaintive warblings in the zephyrs mild,
Thy stronger impulse in the tempest wild,
Thy loudest moanings o'er oppression's wrongs;
And oft have joined, unheard though, in thy song.
    Sing on brave youth, and melt the hearts of men;
With love to aid thee, wield the mighty pen;
Sway all mankind, like reeds before the blast;
Let justice be thy guide, the first and last.
Love yet shall rule the world alone, for love
Will only fit mankind to dwell above.

Let each goddess, sibyl, siren,
   Nymph, or naiad, neriad, muse,
With a wreath of hands environ
   This young bard, and none refuse;
'Round him circle, chanting praises,
   Of the labors of the pen;
Strew his path with bright-eyed daisies,
   Poets are the kings of men.

The Poet.

Weave a crown to deck his forehead,
   Twined alone of evergreen ;
He by men should be adored,
   As the bards of old we 've seen.
Bring the hemlock, cedar, balsam,
   Towering pine and hardy spruce ;
Hasten, gather them for all, some
   Little sprig may bring of use.

Braid the ground pine in a garland,
   With ground ivy, for his brow ;
Intertwine within this marland,
   For this poet of the plow,
Gathered from the rugged mountains,
   Evergreens, in rare design ;
Washed within the Hudson's fountain ;—
   Crown him now, ye tuneful Nine.

   Around me floated, fairy, female forms,
   With drapery white, as trees with winter storms ;
And as each deftly twined, the evergreens to bind
   Me a chaplet of emerald hue ;
   Their voices rose, in grand delighting strain,
   "That poet's labors were not all in vain,"
Then the crown they had made, on my forehead was
   laid
   By the Muses, who gently withdrew.

The Dream.

Among the clouds the vivid lightning flew,
And seemed to tinge them with a darker hue;
The frightened eagle screamed, and wilder fiercer, seemed
    Like the voice of a demon below;
My guests celestial vanished from the scene,
The trampled moss alone showed where they'd been,
But the crown that I wore is a treasure I store,
    Much more rare than could mortals bestow.

I cannot use the language they did speak,
'Twas neither English, German, French nor Greek,
More soft than liquid Latin, more smooth than finest satin,
    As it flowed, fresh and free, from the tongue;
Their music, also, was no earthly sound,
'T was finer far than mortal ever found,
And so sweet in its tone, that the angels alone
    Could surpass it, or Orpheus' song.

A hand like mine is only fit to pen
The thoughts of mortals in the words of men;
I cannot well convey, or properly portray
    The sweet language of goddess or muse,
The heaven-born visions the celestials brought,
Enwrap my soul, absorbing every thought.
Will my friends forgive me, for translating so free,
    And the errors of writing excuse?

The Poet.

Sam shrugs his shoulders, mutters " mebby so,"
    And Nick assumes a half suspicious look;
Cæsar looks frightened, and proceeds to go
    Back to the kitchen, and prepare to cook
The morning meal, as usual; trout and venison.
The rest prepare for sleep's refreshing benison.

Says Sam, " Poeta, have you ever climbed
    Over the rocks in Adirondack pass?
It seems to me," and Samuel almost rhymed,
    " That your description would be called first-class.
No poet's pen can do full justice to it.
Those who desire to see it, they must "' do it.' "

Says Nick, " Poeta, wa' n't them Indian girls
    That danced around you, and half set you crazy?
If you should see St. Regis' maids in curls,
    I 'll bet your heart would not beat half so lazy;
If you should feel the lightning from one's eye,
You 'd snap as quick as trout do for a fly."

To bed, or bunk, the sleepy party creep,
    Their raiment hanging from projecting knots
In indistinctness melts; at length a heap
    Of phantoms weird appear in divers spots;
The timid breeze just sways them to and fro,
And makes them life-like in the camp-fire's glow.

Chronicle.

A little screech-owl, startled by the light,
  Awakes the echoes with unearthly yell;
A voice demoniac adding to my fright,
  But breaking up the terror of the spell,
Now flutters round our cabin dark and wild,
And shrieks vociferous as a spunky child.

How any one should think that owls were wise,
  That have to get their knowledge in the dark,
Creates in me a feeling of surprise,
  That they should e'er be thought to have the mark
Of wisdom round them; do n't each farmer know
They have not half the wisdom of the crow.

Ah! now sweet sleep has settled on each friend,
  And through this lonely vale deep silence reigns;
The hopes of youth the facts of manhood blind,
  And weave a web in dreams in all their brains;
With pictures bright and gay, and dun and sober,
As spotted as a forest in October.

Within the kitchen is a loud dispute,
  The guides and cook are growing rather warm,
For Sam contends that men can't be half brutes
  Like fawns and satyrs, nor assume their form,
Which Nick denies, contending rather plucky
That men are called half horse in old Kentucky.

The Poet.

"I think I know a heap about these goddesses,
  I've seen their images in York and Boston
As white as snow," said Cæsar, "and how odd it is
  The less they're dressed, the more they're apt to cost one.
They could not live up here, they would be frozen,
For those I saw had not a rag of clothes on.

"I've seen some pictures in the Almanacs,
  Where handsome ladies floated in the air,
Or riding flying horses on bare backs,
  With trailing robes, and crowns and flowing hair,
Without a bit of bridle, girth or saddle,
  But out of fashion with your modern fair,
Just like our Indian maids who ride astraddle."

At length their clack is deadened by the brook
That ever trills its silver sounding chime;
  The breeze just sighs within our quiet nook,
But on the mountain wakes a chord sublime;
  Its echo dies, a sweet and sad refrain,
By forests softened, or through rocky rime,
  As distance mellows oft the ocean's strain.

CHAPTER IV.

THE ENGINEER.

Chronicle.

To-day we made a sort of grand excursion,
    We traced the river up to beauteous Colden,—
A little lake,—and felt a slight aspersion
    Beneath a cascade's dashing, flashing, golden
Water, that, colored by a recent rain,
Where e'er it touched us, left a dirty stain.

We saw Lake Avalanche, a pretty pond,—
    No doubt 't was formed by mighty mountain slide,
We crawled through trap dykes; we are rather fond
    Of penetrating thus the mountain's side.
We'd like to go through Marcy, were we able,
As we have Palmer Hill, on the Ausable.

Three thousand feet above the deep blue sea;
    Three thousand feet up in etherial blue:
Above us still the mountains rising free,
    With caps of hazy, misty, leaden hue,
That cling like politicians to the spoils;
To men, old habits; odors unto oils.

The Engineer.

We found high-poised a mighty, clinging mass,
    Just ready for a topple, and we wondered
If human strength inertia could surpass,
    And tried it once; oh, how it fairly thundered,
Rolling and bounding, crashing through the trees;
There's boyish pleasure still, in feats like these.

We sent some little boulders whizzing, flying
    Into Lake Colden, with a mighty splash;
We sought the Hudson's highest source, and, trying
    To scale a rocky wall, were somewhat rash;
We got, at length, where we had had no business,
And came near falling with a sudden dizziness.

We found rare shrubs, and several autumn flowers
    So rare that none knew aught about their names.
Fine mosses grew without the aid of showers,
    Beneath o'erhanging rocks, with eyes like flames.
A trailing vine that grew the rocks between,
With berries bright as those of wintergreen.

There was not one, I 'm sure, in all the party,
    Including guides, but learned something to-day;
They all enjoyed the tramp, and ate so hearty
    Of pork and beans, and moistened oft their clay
With water from the Hudson's highest spring,—
Fit for a poet, and indeed a king.

Chronicle.

'T is twilight hour; the sky is red as flame
   Far in the west, but overhead 't is yellow;
Sam says, and he to prophecy lays claim,
   "Before the dawning day the wind will bellow."
We hope it will; 't would be a lucky joke,
If it would clear the atmosphere of smoke.

The speaker for the hour's a curious chap,
   His tongue can rattle like a fanning mill;
His mind is active, never takes a nap,
   And roams at random, uncontrolled by will.
He'll talk to you without the least intention
Of stretching truth, and call his tales invention.

There's scarce a great discovery in arts,
   Or in mechanics, that he has not read.
The queerest compound of component parts,
   Seems thrown together in his little head.
A triple mind in this one seems to enter,—
An Engineer, Mechanic, and Inventor.

Beside these, he is something of a rhymer;
   Rhymes flow as easily from off his tongue.
As water from a duck; he's quite a climber,
   At least gets highfalutin; and among
A crowd of people there is not a doubt
Would be called clever; let us hear him spout.
IV.

The Engineer.

Iron Ore.

This bit of brilliant, black magnetic oxyd,
Is but the symbol of enlightened nations;
Deprive them of it, they would slowly settle
Again to savages, and homeless wander,
   So helpless and wretched, so weak and forlorn,
   Their clothing but skins of wild beasts of the wood,
   Their weapons but clubs, or the stone in a sling;
   With implements wood, and utensils of shells;
Groping in blind intellectual darkness,
Hopeless, in ignorance deep and chaotic;
Knowledge would cease of the arts economic,
Commerce would fail, and the wealth of the people.

Though now standing like mountains secure
In their glory that none could deny,
They could fall and to earth be unknown,
With the ease that a cloud fades from view
   When passing the crest of a mountain,
   And drops in a torrent of crystals,
   Which vanish on touching the verdure,
   And sink into uttermost darkness.
Iron and steel but annihilate,—
Far in the depths of the wilderness,
Men would be roaming continually,
Mourning the loss of a paradise;
   The earth would be a dreary, weary waste,
   And man in knowledge scarce above the beast.

The Age of Stone.

When stone was used for arrow heads and axes,
And man, nomadic, roamed the steppes of Asia;
When food and clothing were obtained of cattle,
And warlike weapons from their bones were fashioned,
  The arts and the sciences hid in the gloom,
  With letters and learning completely unknown;
  Tradition the vehicle only of law
That ruled them and kept them attached to a king,
Basely they'd follow the beck of a despot;
Cringing would kneel in submission before him;
Joining his numberless hosts in the conflict;
Dying heroic for king or for country.

Though they fell on the field of the slain,
And in glory their brows were becrowned;
When their souls left the earth for the skies,
It was honor as precious to them
  As laurels bestowed on the living,—
  When dying, to know that their valor,
  Extolled by the bards of the nation,
  A legacy was for their children.
Only a mite of the multitude,
Sinking to earth in its littleness,
Greater in death in its usefulness,
Feeding the soil with the sacrifice.
  Then human life was cheap, a trifling thing,
  Thrown in the scale by some ambitious king,

The Engineer.

The flinty hatchet of the sturdy woodman,
Whose heavy task within the shady forest
Would scarce suffice to fit the needed fuel,
Which daily food required within his household.
   The husbandman tilling his acres of corn, [trees,
   With plows formed of thongs and the branches of
   That rooted like swine in the unyielding sward,
   Must needs have a bountiful crop to repay.
Shepherds their flocks watched on evergreen pastures,
Sheared them with stones rendered rough on their edges,
Carding or combing the wool in their fingers,
Twisting and weaving the thread into blankets.
When a king made a journey from home,
In pursuit of a foe, or a wife,
His unvarying guide was the sun,
O'er the trackless and desolate waste.
   In passing the course of a river
   Too deep for his lengthy-legged camel
   To wade in with comfort or safety,
   No boat nor a bridge gave him passage
Nearer its source he must fathom it,
Where in its greater velocity
Over the rocks or the cobble stones,
Footing was found in security.
   The hunter killed his game with dart of stone,
   And fish were captured with a crooked bone.

The Age of Stone.

Around the earth, wherever man had dwellings,
In ev'ry clime, the relics of their labor
Remain to us in perfect form, as fashioned
By their rude hands back in the depth of ages.
    The plains of old Asia afford them to-day;
    The sands of the Nile have inhumed them with care;
    The lakes of the Swiss so preserved them, they still
    In beauty of finish have lost not a line.
Far in the North, where the country is icy,
Hatchets and spear-heads abound in great plenty;
Iceland and Norway, in Lapland and Russia,
England and Ireland, Sweden and Denmark.

In the land of the West they are found
By the shores of the great chain of lakes,
By the margin of rivers, on hills,
And the prairie's broad emerald breast.
    In Mexico, land of the Aztecs;
    In Peru, the home of the Incas;
    The Islands, the gems of the ocean,
    All yield them in wondrous profusion.
Earth once was peopled with savages,
Living where'er it was possible;
Leaving their relics behind for us
Over them vainly to speculate.
    From roaming tribes, the nations all have grown,
    As bronze and iron supersede the stone.

The Engineer.

On Iran's plain, his flock a shepherd guarding
At night, observes a flash of light from heaven,
And hears the whistle of a meteor falling;
In marshy earth it strikes, and steam arising,
   Reveals unto him its position so sure,
     That planting his crook by the hole in the ground,
     Affrighted he flies to the tent of the priest,
   Invoking his aid in the direful event.
He in a rage from his slumbers so broken,
Priestly in knowledge of men and their passions,
Sees that the shepherd with fear stands and trembles,
Telling his tale of the flight of a demon.

It is morn; they repair to the spot
And commence to exhume from the pit
That they find in the moist spongy soil—
Not a demon itself, but its egg.
   So lately, too, has it been laid there,
   'T is warm with an odor of sulphur;
   So heavy it scarce can be lifted
   From where it so deeply is buried.
Here, to the priest, is a mystery;
This is the nit of some deviltry;
Surely he soon must deliver it;
Fire on the altar must conquer it;
   The tribe assemble, quite a little host,
   To see the new-laid egg of demon roast.

Discovery of Iron.

Upon the earthen altar fire is flashing,
The blazing fuel gives out heat intensely;
Around the heavy egg that, incandescent,
Yet holds its form, nor breaks, nor melts; emitting
  Its sulphurous vapors, convincing the priests
  Its origin evil; unharmed by the fire,
  A positive evidence 't is of its birth;
  This devil incarnate must needs be destroyed.
Calling to aid them the hammers of blacksmiths,
Striking with stones on this spawn of a monster,
Banging and bruising, they make but two pieces,—
Toil till they sink with fatigue on the greensward.

Now the shepherd most loudly proclaims
That the stone is the gift of the sky,
And designed by the ruler above
As a point for the nose of the plow.
  The king of the tribe needs a falchion;
  His words by the blacksmiths are heeded;
  They fashion the shepherd his coulter,
  And sword for the king of their country.
War, with its evil trains numberless,
Follows the flash of the scimetar;
Empires arise and man's destiny
Follows the plow in futurity.
  And thus it was, from out the savage state,
  Mankind arose with iron to be great.
IV.

The Engineer—The Smith.

The Scythian's god, a sword; it was of iron,
And sacrifices oft were made unto it;
The Spartans coined their iron into money,
But not as Plutarch tells, the real reason,
    Its rarity, made it more precious than gold
    For bracelets of queens and the crowns of the kings;
    E'en during the reign of King Edward the Third,
    His kettles and pots with his jewels were classed.
Romans invading the vales of Helvetia,
Conq'ring the resolute tribes of the Norman,
Sweeping with vengeance the Saxon and Briton,
Came with the sword and with weapons of iron.

In dark ages the smith was a knight,
And was ranked as the next to the king;
Even poets sang songs in his praise,
And the ladies becrowned him with flowers.
    The magical sword had a power
    That bronze could or did not inherit;
    Its flash, like the darting of lightning,
    Could liberate princess, enchanted.
Sword of King Arthur, "Excalibur,"
Rings on the romance of chivalry;
Vulcan and Thor in mythology
Ranked and revered were as demigods;
    Through centuries weary of progressive stage,
    Mankind have wandered in the Iron Age.

Iron Age.

Now, iron has become so universal,
There's not a trade, or art, or occupation
But some way uses it; the farmer, shepherd,
And each mechanic of the hundred species.
  In slenderest wire, or the shaft of a ship,
  The cable, the rigging, the anchor, the hull,
  The lightning conductor, the whaler's harpoon,
  The press of the printer, the engine, the rail.
Engineers, daring the gorge of Niagara,
Span it, like spiders, with webbing of iron;
Laying their tubes o'er the mighty St. Lawrence,
Tying with cables the two worlds together.

From the day of our birth to our death,
In the cradle or coffin confined;
In the galleries under the sea,
Or balloons that arise in the air;
  In palace or prison we find it;
  At birth in the doctor's prescription;
  Certificate given in marriage,
  Or wills of the dead,—all are iron.
Who has the time to enumerate
Even a tenth of its usefulness?
Mathematicians can calculate
Hardly a tithe of the wealth in it.
  Mankind progresses, and we daily feel
  We're just beginning on the Age of Steel.
IV.

The Engineer—Age of Steel.

'T is *steel* that tips the pen of kingly poet,
It forms the bases of the painter's colors ;
The chisel, rasp, and scraper of the sculptor;
The architect's scale, the square, dividers.
    Perfection of motion, a lady on skates ;
    The strings of pianos; of music the key;
    The tools of engravers, and also the plate ;
    The curves of the gardener, his angles and lines;
Commerce is guided by mariner's compass;
States are surveyed, and the contents are measured;
Steel for the principal parts of our railroads,
Soon will be bridging the Father of Waters.

Then the guns in our forts will be steel,
And with steel will our forts all be clad ;
And the monitors roving the sea,
Will be steeled against stealing of foes.
    'T is steel that now governs all watches ;
    The surgeon who uses the lancet ;
    The punch for the type-founder's matrix ;
    The key to the shaft of a steamer ;
Lines in astronomer's instruments,
Finer than eye can distinguish there;
Shafts that the oaks would deem brotherly,
Wrought are, with care and facility ;
    The olden king from his high place is hurled,
    And Steel, triumphant, rules the rising world.

Inventions.

The great discoveries, and the grand inventions,
That stand as epochs in the growth of nations,
Would all be nought, if only steel were lacking.
The printing press, the world's all-moving lever,
  The engine of commerce, the motor and guide;
  The spindles and looms that provide us with cloth;
  The reaping of grain, or the grinding of food;
  The ginning of cotton, the sewing machine.
Telegraphs would ne'er have had an existence;
Still undiscovered the art of Photography;
Who could have drilled the deep wells,—the Artesian?
Mined for the metals, or drifted a tunnel?

The Inventors of every age,
In mechanics, or physics, or arts,
In the sciences useful and grand,
That contribute to pleasure or gain,
  Have never been fully acknowledged.
  We rarely appreciate genius,
  Especially during its lifetime,
  But over its bones rear a column.
Strike from the world the discoveries
Wrought by the mind's great inventiveness,
Seeking the stone of philosophy,
Striving for motion perpetual,
  The earth would lack its richest, rarest works,
  And Anglo Saxons dwindle to the Turks.

The Engineer—Fiction.

When Homer sang the wrath of bold Achilles,
In plot and detail all of rare invention,
He burst the bonds that bound his fervid fancy,
And roamed at will in rich, romantic regions.
   When Dante created his poem divine,
   And grand inspiration illumined his soul,
   He sailed speculation's tumultuous sea,
   'Mid imagination's most beautiful isles.
Milton from darkness uplifted our language;
Shakspeare made classic the epochs of history;
Bulwer and Scott, with their wondrous inventions,
Please like desserts that should follow a feasting.

In our infancy we all were charmed
With the stories of Old Mother Goose;
And the pictures then formed in our minds
Will outlast the impressions of fact.
   Poor Robinson Crusoe is loved more
   Than Washington, Franklin, or Lincoln,
   By school-boys, who take great delight in
   Arabian Nights Entertainment.
Take from our tongue the romantic part;
Snatch from our poets the fanciful,
Never to tolerate novelists,
Robs us of half of our literature.
   If all our books were history or fact,
   In life's grand drama we should lose an act.

Imagination.

I sometimes have a happy flight of fancy,
And try my skill at quaint and queer inventions;
But thus far find within the Patent Office,
There's always some one just arrived before me.
   A pupil in school, I could varnish a tale,
   Or color a falsehood to look like the truth;
   And, had I been properly trained, could have been
   A novelist sure; but without it am nought.
Schooled in the by-roads of modest invention,
Never a chance to regale in rich pastures,
Rough and uncouth are my creatures of fancy,
Clothed in old-fashioned and ill-fitting garments.

But grotesque as they are in their garb,
And erratic in action and speech,
As they troop through my mind they but leave
The impressions I like to preserve.
   Like sketches first made by a painter,
   A line often times will be careless,
   And needs just the slightest retouching,
   Till matching original nature.
Wait till I weave you a fanciful
Web, thin and light as a gossamer;
Wrought in the quaintest of workmanship,
Flowers of rarest embroidery;
   Allow me, then, to tell my rustic story,
   As some Italian improvisatore.
   IV.

The Engineer—Lay of a Lunatic.

Sunset.

One bright evening in October,
Madam Nature did enrobe her
In a vestment gray and sober,
    Though in beauty o'er her flung;
For the day-king had descended,
And his reign of glory ended,
Yet his lingering rays were blended
    With the clouds that o'er him hung;
        And in gorgeous, golden grandeur,
            To the floating clouds they clung,
        Like two ardent lovers meeting,
        Or a mother to her young.

Soon the sun's uncertain glimmer,
Paler, fainter grew, and dimmer,
And, in absence of their trimmer,
    Darker grew the clouds, and gray;
Wood and field at once grew duller,
Changing, deep'ning in their color,
And the sky with clouds grew fuller,
    Tinged with day's declining ray;
        Much they looked like mourners weeping
            In a melancholy way,
        For the fleeting, changing beauties
        Of a dear October day.

Lay of a Lunatic—Twilight.

Cool the breezes were, and pleasant,
Ever changing, evanescent,
In the west the silver crescent
    Pale and dimly could be seen.
Bright the stars looked down in beauty,—
Heaven's sentinels on duty,—
Where the sky just tinged to suit a
    Painter, seemed to intervene
        In a deeper, darker girdle
            Round, the heaven and earth between,
        And the clouds, like spectres gliding,
        Threw their shadows o'er the scene.

Slowly, sure, the constellations
Duly forming, took their stations
In their usual situations,
    Where for ages they have shone:
O'er the distant western valley,
Yet the lingering moonbeams rally,
Gathering on the hill-tops, dally,
    As though struggling to atone
        For the absence of their mother,
            Whose retiring they bemoan;
        Paler, fainter, fainter, paler,
            Till each lingering ray had flown.

The Engineer—Time.

Time, unnoticed, flew unheeding,
With his pinions nought impeding,
In the grove the breeze was pleading
    With the thief to stay his flight;
But with sorrowful endeavor,
Ever changing, yielding never,
Still old Time flew on as ever,
    Sweeping earth before his might;
        Wheeling onward, rushing, flying,
        Like a limbless. ghastly sprite,
        Till the evening star was waning,
        And proclaimed it near midnight.

Slow the village clocks tolled 'leven,
When across the northern heaven,
Rose a ragged, rough, uneven
    Bow of lurid, lightning glare,
And I never placed my eyes on,
(Or, at least, with such surprise on),
Such a bow in the horizon,
    As the one before me there;
        E'en the glad'ning bow of promise
        To the world's unworthy heir,
        Placed beside this bow of glory,
        Surely feebly would compare.

From this bow that interveneth,
And the little twinklers screeneth,
Shot strange columns to the zenith,
    With a quick, enchanting light;
Flashing, flaming, floating, fleeting,
Whirling, wheeling, marching, meeting,
Rushing, rolling, and retreating,
    Like grand armies in a fight;
        Mighty armies of the heavens,
            With their shields and armor bright,
        Waving plumes and floating banners,
            On the canopy of night.

As the skies grew bright and brighter,
And the earth looked light and lighter,
Then the crimson army whiter
    Grew, and vanished from the scene;
They withdrew so queer and quaintly,
Softly, solemnly and saintly,
Leaving but a trace, so faintly
    That I doubted I had seen.
        Much I marveled at their movements,
            Standing doubtingly between
        Solemn fact and fickle fancy,
            Wond'ring what it all could mean.

IV.

The Engineer.

Suddenly a ray appearing,
Wild and mad in its careering,
Set me trembling then, and fearing,
    Lest it soon might disappear;
And so anxious was my dreading,
That the ground I scarce was treading,
As I saw it slowly spreading
      Over earth's night-shaded sphere;
        When I saw it slowly crowning
        Earth with glowing, golden gear.
      Fairer scene man ne'er beheld yet,
      Neither poet, saint nor seer.

Now unrolling like a banner,
In a rich and tasty manner,
Loosely floating like a lanner
    Calmly watching for her prey;
Now like flaming meteors dancing,
Or a thousand war steeds prancing,
With their burnished armor glancing
    In the gleaming light of day;
      Like the glittering of jewels
        On some sparkling, fabled fay;
      Or the flash of red artillery
      In the battle's stern array.

The Lay of the Lunatic—Aurora Borealis.

Ev'ry glory seemed to enter
To the deepest, dearest center
Of the spirit of th' inventer
    Who reviewed the glorious whole;
And attuned his heart with pleasure,
In the sweetest, choicest measure,
Yielding him the greatest treasure
    Ever welcomed by his soul;
        'T was a frantic freak of nature,
        Round the ice-encircled pole;
        On my memory a beauty
        I was careful to enroll.

Now the flaming lights unbidden,
Flashing steeds by fairies ridden,
From the haunts where they had hidden,
    Rushed half frantic to the fray.
All their movements seemed a riddle,
To my mind a mystic fiddle,
As they pranced along the middle,
    Of the northern milky-way;
        As they flew in flashing splendor,
        Dashing joyously and gay,
        Far across the breadth of heaven,
        In magnificent array.

IV.

The Engineer.

From the heavens remotest tenter,
Ev'ry fairy seemed to enter
On a strife, to reach the center,
    Which most quickly they did do;
For in less than half a minute
From the time they did begin it,
They'd circle formed, within it
    Ev'ry flaming steed withdrew;
    And the center of this halo,
        Tinged with darker, deeper, hue;
    Had around it mighty circles,
        Orange, yellow, green and blue.

Over me, this halo pending,
Slowly, surely, seemed descending,
'Till I thought a tragic ending
    Soon would crush my dearest hope;
Though in beauty bright appearing,
I could plainly see 'twas nearing,
So I wondering stood, and fearing,
    Like a culprit by his rope;
    Standing, fearful of a mighty
        Force, with which I could not cope;
    And from which it seemed as useless
        Of my thinking to elope.

The Lay of the Lunatic—Aurora Borealis.

Round my head it seemed to hover,
And my trembling frame to cover;
There I stood as stands a lover,
    And as anxious for his fate;
But the shadows wrapt around me,
And so intricately bound me,
Fairly seeming to confound me,
    In my weak and nervous state;
        Like the phantoms of an incubus,
        Or deliriously elate;
        And so closely, that beyond them,
        Vision could not penetrate.

Fast my heart was throbbing, beating,
Every nerve that throb repeating,
And my brain, in wild entreating,
    Tried to force my tongue to speech;
Ev'ry muscle in a flutter
At each word I tried to utter,
Still my stammering tongue would stutter,
    Sticking, shockingly in each,
        'Till I found 'twas useless trying,—
        Not a word was in my reach,
        So I ceased my vain endeavors,
        And I tried not to beseech.

The Engineer.

Soon I heard a horrid shrieking,
Half betwixt a howl, or squeaking,
I could scarce believe 't was speaking,
 So unearthly was its tone;
Pitched as high as shrill *falsetto*,
Moving brisk as *allegretto*,
Piercing, like a steel stiletto,
  To the marrow of each bone;
   Like a ragged, jagged arrow,
    'Till I thought my breath had flown;
   Leaving body as a captive
    Unto beings yet unknown.

I at first thought 'twas a gnomen,
For it sounded so inhuman;
Then I thought a half-crazed woman,
 Might produce as harsh a sound;
Soon the voice grew softer, sweeter,
And I thought that I could meet her,
And imploringly entreat her,
  With my knees upon the ground,—
   Beg a respite of my sentence,—
    But it was in vain, I found,
   Like a felon in a pillory,
    Stood amazed and gazed around.

The Lay of the Lunatic—Electricity.

Presently the voice grew nearer,—
'T was a woman, or one dearer,—
I 'd no cause to hate or fear her,
    For so lovely did she seem ;
Bright her eyes with beauty glancing,
Set the blood within me dancing,
For their ray was so entrancing,
    I was stricken with their beam ;
      And my thoughts flew wildly fleeting,
        In a rough and broken stream,
      Like the half-remembered shadows
        Of a vague and fevered dream.

While I thought to thought was linking,
Every look with rapture drinking,
She upsets my train of thinking
    With a heavy, half-drawn sigh ;
And in manner meek as Moses,
To my longing sight discloses,
'Neath her lips like unblown roses,
    Wealth in pearls gold could not buy ;
      Making music at each breathing,
        Fit for mansions built on high ;
      Asking what my humble name was,
        What I wished, as well, and why.

IV.

The Engineer.

I was tongue-tied then no longer,
Feeling resolute and stronger,
"Madame," said I, " I 'm the younger,
    What are your commands with me?"
" No commands have I for you, sir,
There is nothing you can do, sir,
Ask of me, I 'll tell you true, sir,
    I will answer plain and free;
        Fairly ask of known or unknown,
        And it all divulged shall be,—
        Of the earth, or heavens above you,
        Or the secrets of the sea."

Felt I then a decade older,
More important and some bolder,
Finally I tried and told her
    I would like to know her home.
And her birth place, if she 'd known it,
And the reason why she 'd flown it,
If she had eloped, to own it,
    Why it was that she should roam;
        Little dreaming that her mansion
        Was beneath the ocean's foam;
        Quite unconscious she 'd been dwelling
        In the castle of the gnome.

The Lay of the Lunatic—Electricity.

" Where the daring sailor presses,
In his terrible distresses,
'Mid the deep and dark recesses
    Of the gloomy, frozen North;
There I reign in all my glory,
With my heralds grim and hoary,
Who have made a yearly foray,
    As I sent them fiercely forth;
    Variously have I been christened,
    But I never had a birth;
    Eternally I've dwelt within
    The bowels of the earth.

" I am 'Zeus' of the Grecian;
And 'Jehovah' of Phenician;
'Goda' of the true Parsean;
    'Prince of ill' in heathen lands;
The American's 'Great Spirit',
Part of whom all men inherit,
All the living have the merit
    Of the finish of my hands;
    Worlds around, above, below you,
    Are encircled by my bands,
    And I move them all, from Jupiter
    Down to the smallest sands.

The Engineer.

" Life and power to all the living,
To the planets motion giving,
All controlling, ne'er receiving,
    Save a portion of my whole ;
Ruling power of all in nature ;
Ruled by one whose power is greater,
HIM, the Architect Creator,
       Of the universe, the soul.
           But the stars that move unnumbered,
           Are not under my control ;
           I 've a sister at each center
              Of the systems as they roll. .

" For an hour I might be summing
All the grand things that are coming,
When the trains of people humming
    O'er the country by my might ;
When balloons, unheld by tether,
Roam at will in spite of weather,
And machinery, moved by leather,
       Will be thought a novel sight ;
           When the world is educated,
           And my powers are brought to light ,
           Steam will surely slow be counted
              When I fairly claim my right."

The Lay of the Lunatic—Electricity.

"Madam," said I, "you are joking,
This is fun that you are poking,
I should think such things were choking,
　　Though you utter them with ease.
Give me proof; if you have power,
Make for me a single flower;
Can you stop the sun an hour,
　　　Or the planets as you please.
　　　　Something easier at your option,
　　　　Hush this feeble, gentle breeze.
　　　　Change it to a piercing, blighting
　　　　　　Blast, and make this brooklet freeze."

"Laws so fixed and long ordained sir,
Cannot, must not, be profaned sir,
And will always be maintained sir,
　　Throughout all eternity;
Should I make a slight reversion,
Simply for your own conversion,
It might end in some diversion,
　　And in great uncertainty;
　　　　I prefer to leave you doubting,
　　　　　　Than that such a thing should be;
　　　　It might spoil the calculations
　　　　　　Of astronomers, you see."

The Engineer

"Madam," said I, "You can turn a
Lie, as well as an attorney;
Can't you take an airy journey?
   Say for instance to the moon."
"If you think that you can stan' it,
I'll conduct you to each planet,
Giving you some time to scan it,
   Since you ask of me a boon;
     We will start in half a minute,
     If you'd like to go so soon;
     Will you have a coach and six, sir?
     Will you mount as a dragoon?

"Madam," said I, "saint or siren,
Bring your dashing steeds of fire on,
Harnessed well with steel and iron,
   And your strongest, gayest coach;
For in fact I am particular,
Some old maidish, quite a stickler;"
This odd notion seemed to tickle her,
   And she ordered an approach
     Of a span of spanking horses,
      Whose broad wings did quite encroach
     As they brushed along beside me,
     But I offered no reproach.

The Lay of the Lunatic—The Journey.

Off we started in a hurry;
Mind, I did not like the flurry,
But I thought I would not worry,—
  Where she went I sure could go;
I had often dreamed of flying,
Rather, I had dreamed of trying,
'Till I thought my movement vieing
  With the flashing lightning's glow;
    But compared with our velocity,
      All my dreams were dreadful slow;
    Like the light from day-god flying
    On we flew, that's fast you know.

She so freely put the lash on,
In a most romantic fashion,
That like meteors we did dash on,
  'Till I fairly laughed outright;
Mightily was I elated,
As our speed accelerated;
But in fact 't was underrated,
  For so rapid was our flight
    That we reached the planet Neptune,
      Leaving Saturn on our right;
    Nineteen minutes from the starting,
      If I kept the time aright.

The Engineer.

As it lay out-spread before us,
I began to feel dolorous,
For it looked so soft and porous
    That I said " I 'll not alight."
So we slowly flew around it ;
I 've no doubt but I could sound it,
For so gaseous we found it,
    So transparent, thin and light ;
        Then I saw it was inhabited,
        And by many a little sprite,
        " Transcendentalists ?" I whispered,
        And she answered, " you are right."

Sprites like these could not detain us,
So we started for Uranus ;
They could never entertain us
    With a transcendental plea ;
I was sorry we had left it
'Till I 'd had a chance to heft it,
I presume that I could lift it
    Quite as easy as a pea ;
        If I had good ground to stand on,
        There 's a chance that I could be
        Represented as an Atlas,
        Pictured often as you see.

The Lay of the Lunatic—The Journey.

When we reached that destination,
Quick I took an observation,
Merely giving salutation
    To the planets as we came;
On we flew to mighty Saturn,
Looking like a brazen flat urn;
Passing that we reached the pattern
    Planet, Jupiter by name.
        These were covered with the millions
           Who had died unknown to fame,
        On the records of the living,
           Never had the smallest claim.

These three looked both thin and airy,
Like the mansions of a fairy,
So, in fact, I did not care a
    Fig because we did not call.
Saturn's rings were dim and brassy,
All their satellites looked gassy,
Flying round us thick and saucy,
    Insignificantly small,
        And perhaps about as heavy
           As a regulation ball;
        Deserving not so large a name,
           Or of satellites at all.
  IV.

The Engineer.

Next, we passed the little Juno,
And her five score sisters; few know
Half the names of them, but you know
    All about her taking harm;
How a mighty comet hit her,
And provokingly so split her
As to cause a dusty litter,
    And a consequent alarm;
        Till old Orpheus set them waltzing,
        Which they still do to a charm,
        Seeking, maybe, for a squatter,
        Trying to pre-empt a farm.

Here have dwelt for several ages,
Heroes of the various stages,
Whose bright names are on the pages
    Of the histrionic scroll;
Famous singers and musicians,
Noted priests and politicians,
Sages, orators, physicians,
    Dwarfs and giants, jesters droll;
        Martyrs, patriots, philoso-
            phers, philanthropists, the whole;
        All the architects and artists,
            Here together, cheek by jole.

The Lay of the Lunatic—The Journey.

Antiquarians and geolo',
Old grammarians and philolo',
Lexicographers, concholo',
　　Statesmen, monarchs, and divines;
Chemists, painters, and zoolo',
Dramatists and paleolo',
Journalists and icthyolo',
　　Engineers, the skilled in mines;
　　　Paleontolo', entimolo',
　　　Chiefs in their respective lines;
　　　Only those whose deeds surpassing,
　　　Each with name that brightly shines.
　　　*(Can't you see the "gist" is lacking
　　　In the ending of those lines?—P. D.)*

Fiery Mars we reached quite quickly,
Having flown both smooth and slickly;
This appeared to be most likely
　　Of the planets I had seen;
There was something of solidity,
And resembling stern frigidity,
So I lost my late timidity,—
　　Gladly, haply would have been
　　　Then a circumnavigator
　　　Of its cold and brassy mien;
　　　But our time, you know, was precious,—
　　　I'd much knowledge yet to glean.
IV.　　　　　　　　　　　　　　860

The Engineer.

Since the dawn of man's creation,
Warriors here of ev'ry nation,
Tyrants, too, of ev'ry station,
   Kings and princes, sultans, popes.
Emperors and queens, oppressors,
Base, licentious dispossessors,
Cold, unprincipled confessors,
   All misguiders of our hopes.
      Here low murderers and villains,
         Those whose necks deserve the rope,
      Mingled are in wild confusion,
      In one great kaleidoscope.

Off we started, then, for Venus,
Quick we closed the space between us,
You on earth here might have seen us,
   As we passed you in the sky.
No, I grant you quick acquittal,
For the earth looked wondrous little,—
Like a pea beside a kettle,
   Viewed with Jupiter on high.
      Luna looked just like a mustard,
         You could put her in your eye,
      And I like not to have seen her,
      For we flew so swiftly by.

The Lay of the Lunatic—The Journey.

Venus was reserved for ladies;
Here each ancient virtuous maid is,
Who, too pure for earth, or hades,
    Dwells in peace, but not alone ;
Though on earth they 'd hearts of iron,
Which poor cupid dare not fire on,
And the poetry of Byron
    Fell like feathers on a stone.
        Here they 're placed in close communion,
        As though partly to atone,
        With the debauchees and liber-
            tines, the worst the world has known.

As a just and true recorder,
I, of course, proceed in order,—
We were nearing Mercury's border,
    Where I thought it awful hot ;
Much it looked like Ætna's crater;
Here were they whose crimes were greater,
Here it was that dwelt each traitor,
    This was their tormenting lot ;
        They were not a mighty army,
        May be fifty on the spot ;
        Sure their king had lost a pedal,
        And I guess he had been shot.

IV.

The Engineer.

To be regular in my story;
There the sun in all his glory,
Hot, vast, terrible and gory,
    Lay within an instant's flight.
Quick I spake, said I, "I 'd rather
Seek a little cooler weather,
You would singe me like a feather,"
    And at this she laughed outright,
        As she wheeled her flying horses
           From the mystic fount of light,
        Seeking satellite of silver,
           Blushing, blooming, Queen of Night.

My poor pen is weak and puny,
Or in glowing praise of Luna,
I most certainly would tune a
    Stanza in Byronic vein.
Here for ages undivided,
Male and female have resided,
They whom half the world derided,
    They whose labors were in vain;
        Here have found that blest reunion,
        Here have held their peaceful reign,
        In the highest state of pleasure
        That poor spirits can attain.

Hesiod, Homer, Horace, Hermes,
Daniel, David, Donne and Dolces,
Musæus, Menander, Moses,
  Moliere and Mirabeau ;
Linant, Lucian and Lucretius,
Ovid, Otway, Ossian, Orpheus,
Thompson, Tasso, Terrance, Thespis,
  Butler, Byron and Boileau.
    Coleman, Congreve, Corneille,
    Rogers, Richards and Rousseau ;
    Shakspeare, Southey, Scott and Shelley,
    Pollock, Prior, Pope and Poe.

Hopkinson and Hood and Hunter,
Goldsmith, Gray, Gay, Dryden, Dacier,
Coleridge, Collins, Campbell, Cowper,
  Croly, Cowly, Chatterton ;
Moore and Milton, More, Beattie,
Barlow, Blaimer, Burns and Baillie,
Wolfe and Wordsworth, White and Welby,
  Fontenelle, Furguson ;
    Sappho, Seward, Smith and Spenser,
    Phillips, Paine and Phillemon,
    Akenside and Ariosto,
    Alfieri, Addison.

The Engineer.

Agathon and old Bacchylides,
Chaucer, Dante, sweet Ebrilides,
Fuller, Gower, young Hermogenes,
    Irwin, Johnson, Keats and Long;
Montague and Nemesianus,
Osgood, Pindar, curious Quintus,
Ramsay, Shenestone and Theocritus,
    Upham, Virgil, Wolcot, Young,
        Zeno and five hundred others,
        That unto the list belong;
        They whose names on earth are widely
        Known, but can't be wove in song.

Since I've written names so many,
'T is a pity to leave any
Unrecorded, though I've been a
    Fool in searching those few out;
For so harshly do they jingle,
Well I know your ears must tingle
With the rattling, ragged fingle
    Fangle I have been about;
        There we left them in their glory,
        Very happy I've no doubt;
        And we sought the earth, the grandest
        Of the planets on the route.

The Lay of the Lunatic—The Journey Ends.

When I found my trip was ended,
I most blandly condescended,
And with my two pedals bended,
    Thanked her freely for the ride.
Then she vanished from my vision,
Leaving me in indecision,
For her northern home elysian,
    Far across the stygian tide;
        O'er the dark and dreary waters,
        Which mysteriously divide
        All the dead from all the living,
        Ferried to the other side.

If you think this lady fooled me,
Or in common parlance " sold me,"
I will tell you what she told me,
    Maybe at some future day;
Though our trip was evanescent,
'T was decidedly most pleasant,
For her tongue ran quite incessant,
    Telling secrets all the way;
        And among the many thousand
        Things this lady had to say,
        " Poets have to write you know, for
        Plaguey little praise or pay."

IV.

The Engineer.

No whisper breaks the silence that ensues,
   No lisped dissent, or murmur of applause,—
The lips of "Sam, the Doubter," e'en refuse,
   As well as all the others, to pick flaws,—
To their repose my choice companions creep,
Some lie awake, some dream,—but few can sleep.

How sweet old memories rise up in the mind,
   As I recall my most poetic days,
When fancy roamed in freedom, unconfined;
   How oft I trilled my feeble boyish lays
In praise of Nature, or delicious charm
I tried to throw around my father's farm.

Oh, with what zest I joined in boyish sports,
   And tried to add a pleasure to each toil;
My mind made castles, but my body forts,
   The merest earthworks in the fertile soil;
I should say breast-works, trenches, vulgar ditches;
Though unpoetical, an aid to riches.

As I glance backward o'er my boyish visions,
   And count the airy castles I have built,
And note my failures and my indecisions,
   Forgetting, also, all the milk I've spilt;
I laugh at all the burdens I have borne,
And feel as happy as a lamb just shorn.

CHAPTER V.

THE HISTORIAN.

Chronicle.

I've been unwell to-day, I could not jingle,
   I hardly know just what's been going by;
I could not read, nor whittle on a shingle,—
   Too much used up to make a shaving fly;
I've lived, but with unspeculating eyes,
And feebly fought mosquitoes, gnats and flies.

'T is twilight hour, a glorious one at that,
   All we could wish in such a spot as this,
Where themes for contemplation come so pat,
   Or sweet instruction never comes amiss;
We seem to love to linger, learn to listen
The best when stars but feebly, faintly glisten.

The young Historian reads to us to-night
   Some little acts he's culled from history's page;
Has taken pains, no doubt, to write it right,
   And like most writers, will of course engage
That all he tells can be received as truthful;
But he is ready—mind he's very youthful.

The Historian.

Clio, most truthful of Muses, I greet thee.
   Heroes the noblest the world ever knew,
Nameless, forgotten, or lost in tradition,
   Safely preserved by thy wonderful pen.
Where but to thee, and thy ponderous records,
   Holding the treasures, the marvelous deeds
Wrought by the brains of the earlier poets,
   Should we now look for their language divine?
Filled are thy tomes with the grandest inventions,
   Rich in discoveries, teeming with lore,
Mingled with horrors of tyrants atrocious,
   Acts philanthropic and marvelous things;
Noble achievements in felling the forest,
   Tilling, subduing refractory earth,
Doubling the bounties of nature reluctant,
   Cheap'ning, enlarging the sources of life.
Incidents small, or exceedingly trivial,
   Faithfully scored on the tablets of time,
Grow in importance when age dims the carving;
   Moss-covered facts form the base of the tower
Rising majestic, as Prescott or Bancroft
   Adds to the structure the well-fitted stone;
Plain but substantial, an Egyptian obelisk
   Symboled simplicity, smooth and severe,—
Strength and solidity, excellent qualities,
   Give to a structure a ponderous form;
Truth in its nakedness, often obtruding,
   Grows more repulsive the more it is seen.

Invocation.

Clio, assist me in telling my story,
   Give me the facts, and the fancies I 'll bring ;
Truth like an oak in the midst of a meadow,
   Ivy like fiction shall hide its rough form ;
Poets who paint us historical pictures,
   Always to aid them have called on the Nine,
Clothing their facts in the garments of fiction,
   Weaving rare flowers in the intricate web ;
Blending tradition with rumors and records,
   Tinging it oft with mysterious hints,
Doubtful allusions to motives deep hidden,
   Cunning conjectures of things that are lost ;
Rearing their columns in graceful proportion,
   Fitting their stones in most beautiful forms,
Carving their facts, that are rough and unshapen,
   Into a softer and lighter relief ;
Mouldings elaborate, frame their medallions,
   Cornices covered with ornaments rare,
Pediments pictured for fancy's fruition,
   Sculptured with skill to conceal the deceit ;
Rising in grandeur each story successive,
   More and more beautiful seems the design ;
Finer the ornaments grow to the vision,
   Coarser they really are, but the eye,
Cheated by distance, is haply contented ;
   Thus 't is tradition, for truth is received ;
Half our romances, when age makes them mellow,
   We shall receive as historical truths.

The Historian—Introduction.

Nicholas, Cæsar and Samuel have helped me;
    Each in his way has related his facts,
Incidents touching our national history,
    Stories they 've told me I 've woven in verse;
Using their language, their thoughts and expressions,
    Only the measure, that simply I claim,—
Merely the purely mechanical structure;
    Fancies and figures and facts are their own;—
Nick has narrated "The Boston Tea Party,"
    Telling me faithful his grandfather's tale;
Adding the ornaments due to tradition,
    Such as he only could properly tell;
I will relate my old grandfather's story,
    Verified faithful by records in print;
How 't was they captured "Old Ticonderoga,"
    Easily, early one morning in May;
Cæsar revealed me the famed Harper's Ferry,
    Madly fanatical "Raid of John Brown";
Singing his strain with the gift of a prophet,
    Ringing the prelude of slavery's knell;
Sam has rehearsed me the "Downfall of Sumter";
    All which he saw and a part which he was;
Telling precisely the thoughts of a soldier
    Stripped of sophistical blandishments bare;—
These are the stories I tell you; if faulty,
    Give unto romance the part that is due,
Credit the poet with earnest endeavor,
    Only to please you in singing his hour.

Nick's Tradition of the Mohawks.

You who read historic novels, with a look of wonder,
Deeming fiction finer, fairer than the written record,
Roaming in the realms of fancy, filled with heartfelt
 pleasure, [dition,
Know not half the romance hidden in the vague tra-
Handed down by careful chieftains of the ruder nations
Unto those who follow after, and the joy it gives them ;
Thus to be the honored vessel, holding them securely,
So the lapse of years can 't harm them, adding nor
 subtracting,
Faithful storing each relation with minute precision ;
Stories told in fitful language of the deeds of daring,
Cunning, courage, long endurance, fortitude and valor,
That the warriors of the Mohawk dared do for the
 Yankees.
When the tyrant mother country levied hateful taxes,
And the people were resisting in the seaport cities;
Calling loudly for a union of the tribes of people,
Massachusetts and Virginia, joining hands in friend-
 ship, [Georgia,
Asking Hampshire and New Jersey, also feeble
Little Rhoda and the others, till a beggar's dozen
Quickly had responded to the earnest invitation,
Sending resolutions of their firm determination,
Never to acknowledge England's sacred right to tax
 them. [nation,
Then within the Mohawk valley, warriors of our
V. 124

The Historian.

Noble, numerous and valiant, painted for the war path,
Offered in the cause of freedom aid to William Johnson.   [struggle,
But the Irish Knight foresaw the fearful coming
And resolved to aid his country, if she should demand him,   [people,
Hoping that concessions would be granted to the
By the King and Parliament, and peace still bless the country;
Knowing wisely that a conflict bringeth but disaster,
Fearing loss of power and prestige, if for country cheering,   [shouted;
Anxious for estate and treasures, if for King he
Playing neutral; while the fearful storm impending gathered,   horizon;
Rolling dismal, distant thunder, round the dark
Careful not to be involved in any agitation;
Asks our bravest Chiefs to spare him, bids them seek the city,   [duty.
Where the "Sons of Liberty" need them, in an active
Brightly blazed the northern forest with the hues of Autumn;   [climate;
Southward flew the birds of passage, seeking warmer
Squirrels chattered in the tree-tops, leaping 'mong the branches,   [like scissors,
Clipping stems of chestnuts, acorns, with their teeth
Till they rattle on the dry leaves, and the ground was covered;
Lazy ran the little brooklets, quiet in the shadow;

Nick's Tradition of the Mohawks.

Warm the sunlight shone, but dimly, through the
   smoky forest,
And a sleepy silence hovered, even in the corn-fields;
Not a breath of air was stirring; glorious Indian
   Summer. [Hudson,
Ten canoes with warriors laden floated down the
Brown of limb and brave of heart; each a child of
   Nature,
Painted, armed and decorated, ready for the war-path.
Forty warriors slily stealing down upon the city;
When the cooling winds of Autumn breathe upon
   the forest, [whoop,
Waking up the sleepy people with a mimic war-
Roused to find a hoar frost lying on the walks and
   fences, [brought it;
Joking, blame the Indians for it, saying they had
Lying quiet, loose around there, waiting with their
   letter, [Council,
That Sir William Johnson gave them, to the Secret
Find at length the men they seek for; have their con-
   sultation, [ended;
Make agreement to remain there till the quarrel's
Stripping off their arms and war-plumes, washing
   from their faces [spotted;
Paints of divers colors, waving, speckled, striped and
Soon appear in modest costume, civil, stern and sober,
But the town was all excitement, tea-ships were ex-
   pected, [gether;
And the Vigilance Committee called the men to-

The Historian.

On the fifth of drear November, they were all assem-
    bled, [landed."
And resolved most absolutely "tea should not be
Then they warned the harbor pilots with a sudden
    vengeance, [burden,
If they brought the vessels bearing such offensive
Round the Hook and in the harbor; consignees
    affrighted, [tion;
Threw up their commissions wisely, on mature reflec-
Then they gave the Mohawks notice "ever to be
    ready." [the skirmish,
They were there, and more than anxious, eager for
With their plumes and paint pots ready, tomahawks
    and hatchets, [ships anchored.
Thirty days they watched and waited, but no tea-
Then the news came on from Boston, "tea was in
    their harbor," [fragile vessels,
And our warriors weary waiting, launched their
Paddling round the coast all icy, crossing bays and
    headlands,
Often saving miles of water by some little portage;
Guided in their expedition by a Narraganset,
Who in youth had been a runner for the tribes
    surrounding; [harbor,
Knowing all the streams and islands, every cove and
Speaking English pretty freely, Iroquois and Pequot;
Knowing, seemingly by instinct, when at night they
    landed, [them;
Who to ask for food and lodging, for no man refused

Nick's Tradition of the Mohawks.

Five short tedious days they traveled, when the spires
    of Boston,   [their bosoms.
Gleaming in the setting sunlight, gladdened much
    Soon they sought for Samuel Adams; they could
    easy find him,
Every boy in all the city knew where he resided;
Taking pride and pains to show them through the
    crooked alleys,
Marching in the Indian fashion, quiet, stealthy, silent,
Not with drums and bugles sounding; no one would
    imagine,   [the war-path;
From their dress that they were warriors, tramping in
Six long days concealed, divided, posted through the
    city,
So as not to rouse suspicion, with impatience waiting,
Till all legal means were ended, and the tea ship
    Dartmouth,
Twenty days had lain at anchor, and the tea not landed,
Nor returned, should serve a pretext for its sure
    destruction;   [ready.
But the day of days was dawning, and the Mohawks
Bright the morning sun is shining o'er the Shawmut
    hill-tops,
Flashing on the waves of ocean, rippled by the breezes,
Sweeping round the rocky islands in the quiet harbor,
Wafting from a dozen seaports little white-winged
    schooners,

The Historian.

Bearing honest, hardy yeomen, flying to the city,
Thinking that their patriot brothers need their good
  assistance;   [forty,
O'er the hills the farmers march, in groups of five to
Passing little hamlets early, ere the fire light blazes
On the hearth-stones of the village, where the dark
  mechanics,   [and soundly,
Weary with their lengthened labors, sweetly sleep
Rousing at the sound of bugle, snatch the meal of
  morning,
Joining in the straggling columns, hasten into Boston.
  In the city all is busy; ten o'clock is tolling;
Round the old South Church they gather, hundreds
  upon hundreds,   '   [porches,
Filling up the aisles and benches, crowding in the
Hearing this report from Rotch, "the ship's refused
  a clearance;"   [Milton;"
Bid him "seek the Governor then, at his home in
That he may proceed at once upon his voyage to
  London.
  Meeting now adjourns to meet again, and anxious
  thousands   [defiant;
Swarm the city's crooked streets, excited, firm,
Thousands gather now again around the church in
  masses,   [and Hancock,
Anxious listening to the speeches; Quincy, Young
Passing noble resolutions, while an answer waiting;
Hark! a lion is arousing; it is Samuel Adams.

222   V.

Sam Adams' Speech.

Friends, citizens, men ; lovers of liberty ;
Time flies ; the day dies, glowing and beautiful ;
Stand firm for your rights, American Englishmen,
    Names that are dear, and with rights as sacred.
King George at home reigns brutal, tyrannical ; [ly
Lords, dukes and knights kneel weak and submissive-
'Round him enthroned, war seems to be threatening ;
    Now with dissensions we must divide them.

Look! see the Court; friends pleading the cause for us
Brave, firm as earth stand ; every expedient
Urge, holding truth, right, higher than Parliament,
    Kings and their Princes, or Courts and Councils.
Shall we retract, shrink, cowardly whimpering;
Crush hope at birth ? No ! doing and daring will
Still stand like rocks, rough ribbing the mountain side,
    Calmly reposing, and yielding nothing.

Wild, fierce as ocean rolling in majesty,
Kings, Courts may come ; Lords, Commoners, Ministers,
Foam, fret on our shore ; dashed into nothingness,
    Scattered you'll see them, returning silent ;
Arms, armies, forts sink into significance,
When freemen fight bold, striking unanimous ;
Long conflict may come, patiently suffering,
    Grandly contending, still we shall triumph.

The Historian.

Tea-ships are here now; lying at anchor they
Swing with the tide; shall patriots willingly
Three pence a pound tax pay for the privilege,
    Drinking the meanness with servile meekness?
What! land the tea? No! standing for principle,
Who would betray such groveling selfishness?
Rights, sacred rights, hold dear as your liberties,
    Union will strengthen our scattered weakness.

New York responds grand; Jersey, Virginia
Hold high their hands; mild Quakers and Georgians
Fail, falter not now; Hampshire, Connecticut,
    Joining us now with ample forces;
Rhode Island brave greets Delaware, Maryland;
"Stand, stand your ground," North, South Carolina
    say,
Earth rings to-day loud, justly with glorious
    Jubilant patriots' silver voices.

King John, from whom was wrested our liberties,
Bold, brave and bad, had none of the tyranny,
Mean, low and vile; gross, base animosity
    Clinging to cowardly King and Councils;
Shall we be taxed without representatives?
Forced blind to drink cups flowing with bitterness,
Bow meek the neck, yoked into allegiance?
    Only to make of us deeper ground-sills?

Sam Adams' Speech.

No! tax, though light, is faulty in principle,
Men, know and feel that test of your manliness;
Fight, fight 's the word; death rather than slavery;
    Loudly proclaim it among the people;
Blow, blow it winds! Sweep over the continent;
Flash fires at night, from mountain to mountain top !
Roar, cannon, roar in cities and villages!
    Ring it ye bells, from steeple to steeple!

God gives to us hopes higher and holier,
Far more to-day; Lo! dim in futurity
Looms grandly up my country's prosperity,
    Nations are bowing, and blush to see her;
I see beyond life, clearly and brilliantly,
Peace, happiness, wealth dawn on these colonies;
Life-long delight dwells lovingly, hopefully,
    Lingering round in the hearts that free her.

Firm fixed in their hearts, all our posterity
Love, praise the day long sought for a jubilee;
Each year beholds fresh marked anniversary,
    Growing the brighter in future ages;
Day dawns, the bells ring, cannon exultingly
Crash, roar; at eve burn brightly and beautiful
Bonfires, that dim stars high in the firmament;
    Brightest of records on history's pages.

The Historian.

Darkness now has reigned an hour, and o'er the
    silent city   [whirlwind ;
Broods the solemn hush, preceding oft a coming
Rotch, the Quaker, just returning from his trip to
    Milton,   [his speaking,
Seeks the church as Samuel Adams just concludes
Makes report "that all is useless;" "now," says
    Adams, rising,   [country ;"
" Then this meeting can do nothing more to save the
    Loudly rings the savage war-whoop through the
    church's porches ;   [plumed and painted,
Forty Mohawks armed with hatchets, war-clad,
March to Griffin's wharf, escorted by at least five
    thousand ;   [ships,
Siezing boats they quickly paddle over to the tea-
Driving off the crews affrighted, open up the hatches
Taking from the holds the tea-chests, touching nothing
    farther.
Everything is still and quiet ; through the dim-lit city
Not a swinging sign is creaking, neither on a steeple
Turns a groaning vane ; the breezes, hushed in fearful
    silence,   [hearts are
Bring no ripple to the water ; full ten thousand
Beating, footsteps muffled seem, and hardly touch the
    sidewalk ;   [and alleys;
But a curious sound is darting through the streets
Crack! and through a tea-chest's cover rings the
    Mohawk's hatchet ;

Grandfather's Story—Prologue.

Swash! and o'er the vessel's bulwarks drops a broken
  tea-chest;
Crack! and swash! and crack! and swash! each rings aloud alternate, [finished;
Just three hundred forty times, and now the job is
This is simply our tradition told me by my father,
Of his father, who was present as a Mohawk Chieftain.

The song I now will sing to you, the tale that I will tell,
Is how that once most mighty fort, Ticonderoga, fell.
How Ethan Allen and his band, when first the people sprung, [young;
To rid themselves of British rule, and Liberty was
Enforced a march from Bennington, through wood and deep morass, [mountain pass;
O'er sandy plains and rocky hills, through dreary
To reach Champlain and take the lock from off the country's door, [store,
Surprised and took the garrison, the fort with all its
And this without the loss of life, or firing of a gun;
A mighty nation had its birth, when this old fort was won. [England's hills,
The solemn news from Lexington, flew o'er New
And every honest, manly heart with sudden vengeance thrills; [morning air,
All through the land the cry "to arms" rang on the

The Historian—The Alarm.

And roused the patriots from their beds, like lions
    from their lair;   [bugle's thrilling blast,
The cannon's boom, the church bell's clang, the
The gathering call in freedom's cause, were echoed
    far and fast,   [delight,
Till every man within the land, had heard it with
And vowed he'd aid the mother land, or for his coun-
    try fight.   [toiled,
The farmer left his oxen yoked, that in the furrow
Nor changed his suit, but went at once, with garments
    torn and soiled;   [half-felled tree,
The woodman dropped his polished ax beside the
And seized the rifle by his side, and started for the sea;
The blacksmith laid aside his sledge; quick at their
    country's call,   [awl;
The carpenter his saw and plane, the shoemaker his
The tailor, with a coat half-made, stopped not to close
    the seam;   [stream.
The fisherman his half-drawn net abandoned in the
The baker hurried from his shop, his bread but
    partly light,   [for fight;
And went to raising men instead, and arming them
The lawyer bid adieu to briefs, to clients and the laws,
And went to pleading earnestly for freedom and her
    cause;   [the tramp,
The doctor took his well-filled bags, accustomed to
And joined his neighbors and his friends, who
    marched into the camp;   [trod,
The minister of peace proclaimed, as on he campward

Prologue—The Women.

"Resistance unto tyrants is obedience to God;"
And every man that had a heart, that had the strength
   to go,   [meet the foe.
His knapsack shouldered, and his gun, and rushed to
The women seized the implements their husbands
   had to leave,   [to rest or grieve,
And breathed a brief, but ardent prayer, nor stopped
But drove the oxen in the field, before the uncouth
   plow,   [sive cow,
Or yoked the odd, unbroken steer with some submis-
Or harnessed up the untamed colts, unused to tug or
   rein,   [rowed in the grain
And hitched them to a half-trimmed crab, and har-
They sowed the turnips and the flax, they planted
   beans and corn,
By them the logs and brush were burned, the sheep
   were washed and shorn,   [rolls were spun
The wool was carded by their hands, by them the
And wove, and into garments made, to clothe a sire
   or son;   [swords,
They burnished up old epaulets, and polished rusty
And scraped to lint their paper-rags, destroying thus
   their hoards,   [prudent wife,
Which they had saved to purchase tea, for then each
Obtained with almost useless things the luxuries of
   life.   [promotes,
No sacrifice is deemed too great, if it the cause
They gave for cartridges for guns, their flannel
V.   petticoats,   370

The Historian—The Gathering.

Besides a thousand other things, and did them as they ought,   [husbands fought.
To aid their own dear native land, while sons and
The rocky hills that cluster round the head of Lake Champlain,   [worldly gain,
Have reared a race of hardy men, unblessed with
But men whose frames are like the rocks, unsheltered from the storm,   [pure and warm,
Whose minds are just as true as steel, whose hearts are
Who hate a wrong in any shape, and dearly love the right,—   [fight;
Are ready with the purse or sword to aid it in a
To suffer hunger, heat and cold, toil, penury and strife,   [blood or life.
For freedom for a continent, though bought with
And such have met at Bennington, a curious motley throng,   [eighty strong,
Undrilled in camp, unskilled in arms, and less than
Who've left their homes upon the hills, and all their household joys,   [Mountain Boys;
To go where Ethan Allen leads the brave Green
James Easton second in command, Seth Warner next we know,
They dare to lead in any place, where any dare to go,
For every face is bright with joy, and every heart beats high, |Fort Ti."
When first informed they are to try to capture "Old

Grandfather's Story—The March.

The roads are rough, the way is long, yes, full one hundred miles,
But silently o'er hill and plain, each company defiles;
The march is forced, but heeding not the toilsome weary way, [lengthy day,
Refreshed by food, but not by rest, throughout the
They make no halt at even-tide, nor till the night's full noon,
Has rendered it imperative, by late descending moon.
Then each encamps to suit himself, like cattle strewn around, [naked ground.
These new made soldiers take their rest, upon the
But when the morning streaks the east, refreshed is every one, [sun;
And ready to resume the march and greet the rising
And all this day they still press on, till just at close of night, [sight.
The village spire of Castleton, becomes a welcome
'Tis here but for a day they rest, in planning their surprise, [of spies,
And posting scouts upon the road, to stop the flight
Till every man his duty knows, and every thing is planned, [take command.
When Arnold comes from Boston, and attempts to
The indignation in the breasts of these brave soldier men, [pen;
Can better be imagined than described by tongue or

The Historian.

For though he is distinguished in the French and
    Indian wars, [scars,
Has for his country risked his life, has to his honor
Has bravery, daring, skill, combined with knowledge
    of the field, [not yield :
Their honest, simple, manly hearts, their leader will
And so announce in warlike phrase, which his high
    hope destroys,
That " none but Ethan Allen leads the brave Green
    Mountain Boys." [no thanks,
But undiscouraged by repulse from those he owes
He volunteers to go with them, a private in the ranks,
Inspired with patriotic zeal, "his country and her
    cause," [applause.
Above a name, a soldier's fame, or the whole world's
The plan's matured, and on the hills young Herrick
    can be seen, [Skene;
With thirty men upon the march, to capture Major
While Captain Drylas northward flies, to Panton, and
    both take [the lake,
The safest means to capture boats and bateaux on
And bring them safely as they can, and each his best
    will try, [enough Fort Ti,'
While night permits, to beach them, and just near
That Allen and his little band may cross the muddy
    strait, [gate,
Between Mount Independence and Ticonderoga's

Grandfather's Story.—The Fortress.

Two tedious, toilsome days they march, each night a
   cold bivouac,   [attack.
Awaking from the last, they see the fort they must
It is the glorious tenth of May, in seventeen seventy-
   five,   [hive
The woods across the lake from "Ti" are busy as a
With half-armed men, whose hands and hearts are
   eager for a fray;   [way.
But scarce a boat can be obtained to cross the watery
For Herrick has not yet arrived, and Drylas is not
   here,   [fast with fear.
And hearts that long beat high with hope, are beating
The day now just begins to dawn, no moment to be
   lost,
For only eighty-three, beside the officers, have crossed.
   Above the waves of Lake Champlain, high on a
      point of land,
The frowning massy walls of old Ticonderoga stand,
A place by nature rendered strong, still stronger by
   each art   [impart.
That gold can purchase, wit contrive, or genius can
In point of engineering skill the first in all the land,
Except one point, and that one point this fortress
   does command,—   [Fort Ti',
'T is Mount Defiance on the south, that looms above
In distance some three thousand feet, and seven hun-
   dred high.
V.

The Historian.

The ramparts on the landward side are earthworks faced with stone.
Then comes a ditch both deep and broad, well filled as it is known, [or shell
And next, the heavy limestone walls, on which a shot
Would be as harmless in effect as though it never fell. [fend
The angles of the curtains have their bastions to de-
The walls from being mined, or scaled; for raking end to end, [iron hail
The guns are placed and ready charged, to send their
With deadly force on any foe that dares them to assail.
Upon these battlemented walls, a hundred guns in place, [command embrace,
Each rood of lake, each rod of land, with dread
While in their rear above them all, the mighty bar-racks stand, [grand
Almost a fortress in themselves, of stone are built so
That none but heaviest of shot their solid walls can harm, [least alarm,
And o'er the whole the lookout stands, to sound the
While in the bowels of the earth, and no way to be seen,
Are dug the mighty storehouses and powder magazine.
Its armament and stores include one hundred twenty guns,
One mortar, fifty swivels, and of musket balls ten tons;

Grandfather's Story—The Attack.

Some thirty new gun carriages, well made for rough-
     est roads,   [loads;
Enormous quantities of shell, of flints three full cart
Of boat building material, a mighty warehouse full,
Of powder, muskets, clothing, food, a store most
     bountiful;   [grounds,
So amply has it been supplied, with such extensive
It cost the British Government, 'tis said, a million
     pounds.   [his boys,
Upon the beach, below the fort, brave Allen and
In silence stand, his half-hushed voice the stillness
     thus destroys: [power,
" Soldiers, you 've long the terror been of arbitrary
" Your valor, that is famed abroad, must yet be proved
     this hour;   [surprise,
" For we must now advance and take this fortress by
" Or quit our vain pretensions, ere the morning's sun
     shall rise;   [wicket gate,
" For I will walk before you, and go through the
" To win a soldier's glory, or to meet a soldier's fate,
" And inasmuch as it is known a desperate attempt,
" Which none but brave men undertake, all others are
     exempt;
" I urge it not on any one 'to stand the battle's shock,'
" So he that now will volunteer, may poise his fire-
     lock;"   [a poise,
And every man within the ranks his gun brings to

The Historian.

Thus hand to hand, and heart to heart, stand these
    Green Mountain Boys.   [toward the fort,
The low commands are given them, they march
And silently and stealthily they reach the sally port;
The sentry snaps his old fusee, by chance it misses
    fire;   [with ire;*)*
*(*Brave Allen rushes on the man, with face suffused
Then fleeing through the covered way, not knowing
    what to do
Until upon the main parade, he gives one wild halloo,
But Allen, Arnold, Easton, these are close upon his
    heels,   [way reveals;
For morning light now breaking forth, his darkened
They quick emerge within the walls, and ere the
    rising sun   [Fort "Ti" is won.
Proclaims the day, they give three cheers, and old
    Now Allen of the sentry asks that he be shown the
    face   [De Laplace;
Of his old friend, now new-made foe, commandant
Who being found, he summoned him who has had
    chief control,   [whole;
To yield to him the garrison, or he'd destroy the
As Captain De Laplace came forth, with breeches in
    his hands,   [demands.
"Surrender me this fortress, sir," bold Allen now
" By whose authority do you demand it, sir," he cries,
" In the name of Great Jehovah and Congress," he
    replies.

498   V.

The Capture.

Reluctantly he's forced to yield, unused to war's
   alarms,
The order gives "to have the men paraded without
   arms;"   [noise,
And thus this bloodless victory, with little useless
Is won by Ethan Allen and his brave Green Mountain
   Boys.   [rious scene,
How splendidly the sun comes up to gild the glo-
A brighter day for this fair land there never yet has
   been;   " sea to sea,
They drink success to Congress, and in hopes from
That this fair land shall yet be rich, be happy and be
   free."

Interlude.

In long, unrequited, degrading, unmerciful bondage,
A RACE had been held by the force of a Christianized
   people;   [Scott Decision,"
The midnight of slavery was reached in the " Dred
And dawning of freedom for millions must certainly
   follow;   [for it,
  Dark, deep, shrouded in gloom, twinkled no star
  Twilight wakens the birds' carol of liberty.

The Historian.

This climax of wrong and oppression awoke the be-
　　nighted,　　　　　　　　　　　　　　　　[ocean ;
Benevolent hearts, that were scattered from ocean to
The sparks of the fire, that would light up a nation
　　in glory,　　　　　　　　　　　　　[the conscience ;
Were struck by the steel of the Court on the flint of
　　Firm hearts, bowing in grief, faithful to principle,
　　Spring back, fearfully quick, with elasticity.

Though thousands regretted this culminate act of
　　the nation,　　　　　　　　　　　　　　　　[sion ;
And yielded before it with quiet and silent submis-
A few, in their hearts, dared to hope that the weight
　　of the burden
Would weaken the back, till unable to carry it safely ;
　　True men never despair, clouds may float over
　　　　them ;　　　　　　　　　　　　　　[bend to it.
　　Huge oaks, stemming the blast, break but ne'er

Its wrongs are too fresh in our minds to require a
　　recital,　　　　　　　　　　　　　　　　　[value,
The struggle too lately concluded to judge of its
The blessings conferred and the cost can 't be weighed
　　in a balance,　　　　　　　　　　　　[fect in healing ;
Till time has revolved, and the wounds shall be per-
　　Fierce war never is healed, leaving no cicatrix,
　　Minds warped, sullen and cold, change but re-
　　　　luctantly.

Interlude.

The spark that enkindled a blaze, till with wild con-
 · flagration, [country,
The demon of battle swept over the breadth of the
Enshrouding its millions of people in direst confusion,
Entombing its thousands in tenements narrow and
 bloody, [the
Lay long dormant and dead; but like the flash of
Quick, sharp lightning it flew, terribly, venge-
 fully.

A pebble but tossed in a pool, with only a splash that
 is noticed, [on circle,
Forgotten the moment 't is over, is followed by circle
And larger and larger they grow, until all of the
 surface [border;
Is rippled with delicate waves to the shelly-bound
Small deeds, earnestly done, move in futurity,
Great things often the more, being so trivial.

The deed of one man, that could make a whole conti-
 nent tremble, [responsive;
Vibrated the chords in the hearts that were beating
The thrill in the nerves, that revolts at a deed most
 atrocious, [tice.
Was painfully felt in the frames of all lovers of jus-
One man ringing the knell fearlessly, bravely the
Key-note sounding on high, over America.

The Historian.

Unmindful of life, or the cost to secure it its freedom,
A bold but fanatical, brave but undisciplined fighter,
Upheld by the faith in the "God that decideth the battle," [righteous,
And firmly believing the cause was most holy and
Fought, bled, proving his faith, shouting triumphantly; [triot.
John Brown died for the race, martyr and pa-

Cæsar's Narrative.

My life had been one long unceasing toil,
No ray of hope broke through my clouded sky;
I felt my bonds grow stronger day by day,
And cutting to my soul; increased desire
To break them racked my brain; I often saw
My fellow free, and had uncertain hints
Of brighter lands where labor earned its gold;
And gold brought comforts, homes and family ties,
That never could be broken, save by death.
  Perhaps the white blood running in my veins
Increased the fond desire I had to learn
To read and write. I only knew enough
To comprehend the picture on the fence
Of some poor colored chattel like myself,
With stick and bundle on his shoulder flung,

Cæsar's Narrative.

And leaning forward, as though in a run;
I knew, or seemed to know, that one had fled
To that far land of hope; then why not I?
My sister, bright and beautiful as morn
When pinkish clouds announce the coming sun,
Was sold to some rich planter farther south;
For what I only guessed; she was too fair
And frail to labor in the cotton field;
Another girl, as fair and slim as she,
Had set tobacco plants beside me days,
And weeks together we had plied the hoe,
And chatted softly; how her wistful eyes
Did longing look whene'er they met my own,
As slily I assisted on her row;

For her sake then, I dared to make attempt
To find the northern lakes, as much to save
Her form from some polluting planter's touch,
As to rejoice in freedom's blessed land.
We fled like fools, and only knew the way
By night when bright the northern dipper shone;
We traced the Shenandoah's fruitful vale
Five weary nights, then stole a skiff to cross
A mighty stream, and fled through woods and fields
Till nearly morn, when suddenly a man
Commanded "halt!" oh, how my heart did beat.
But soon assured that he was much my friend,
We went with him where many men were met,

The Historian.

And joined our fates and fortunes with their own.
　That night I listened unto old John Brown;
His speech sank deeply in my mind; I wish
That better justice could be done to it,
But you 'll excuse the treachery of years.

John Brown's Speech.

　I stand to speak to you; oh, that my voice
Could now resound throughout this lovely land
In thundering tones, far louder than the roar,
The deafening roaring of the ocean's wave;
Till guilty men could hear the solemn truth,
And feel its power within their inmost hearts.
Would that my rostrum now was on the peak,
From whence the sparkling Allegany flows,
And you, my friends, the anxious list'ning hosts,
The thirty millions of our native land.
　The recent outrage on the rights of man
Has kindled in my breast the latent spark
That has been slumbering for years, half dead.
A fire is raging in my inmost soul,
A living fire that only death can quench,
And wrongs inflicted on a fellow-man
Add fuel freely to the flashing flame;
But thoughts like these relieve me of a load

That soon would bow me to the naked earth;
The hearts that beat in sympathy with mine
Relieve my grief and double every joy.

If GOD ordained that man should be a slave,
Why did HE plant within the human breast
That love of freedom which we all have felt?
Why give him, too, a mind to feel the curse,
The deep disgrace that rankles in his soul?
Let those who will defend the curse of Ham,
And call the institution " GOD ordained";
To me, it did not emanate from HIM.
No! man alone must bear the wrath of him
Who feels for millions of his fellow-men,
And wants to act upon the golden rule.
But if we take the Bible for a guide,
In strict accordance with Mosaic law,
We find a sanction for the damning deed.
But happily for us in Christian times,
We seek for reason, justice, love and truth,
And base our claims upon a " higher law"—
A law Divine of Universal Right.   [curse,

Five thousand years have passed since Canaan's
Still earth is peopled by a race of slaves,
And not a sun has climbed the eastern hills
But that a million prayers, from sorrowing hearts,
Have risen pleading for redress from wrong.
His laws are fixed; HE changes not; to-day

The Historian.

HE ever was and ever yet will be
The same through all eternity; 't is well.
Shall we appeal to HIM to lend HIS aid
In such a cause—" the freedom of all men"?
Shall we invoke His blessings on our arms?
Shall we put trust in HIM, or in ourselves?
We 've sent our heralds pleading to HIS throne,
A Howard, Holley, Wilberforce and Sharp,
And yet the curse of slavery still exists;
Is it HIS will? does HE permit the wrong?
Alas! too many justify that view;
Too few against this theory rebel;
" We trust in HIM who doeth all things well."

'T is naught to us how slavery came; 't is here;
We 've naught to do with those who think it right,
They pass for better Christians far than we.
But let us talk of those who think it wrong,
But never show it by their words and deeds.

We all have hearts; we all have friends, we hope;
How should we feel to see a friend a slave,
And dragged from home his wife and little ones,
And doomed to pass his few remaing days,
Amid the swamps in pestilential climes,
Where dread malaria floats upon the air,
And gaunt disease in every stagnant stream?
We 've not the power to picture such a scene;
'T is not a warrior's task; philanthropists,

Narrative — John Brown's Speech.

Those roses of the desert as they are,
Have told us oft in language strange and true,
Of wrongs and woes in half a thousand shapes
That are inflicted on poor Afric's sons.
Why is it thus? have we not heard the wail
That has been sounding through our guilty land?
Have men no minds, and mothers lost their hearts?
Have maidens ceased to love, and man to hate,
That they should cease to speak of such a crime?
No! Heaven forbid! they have not ceased to feel,
Their hearts are much too full for utterance.

Oh! boasted " Land of Liberty !" thy sires
Have filled ignoble graves, thy baser sons
Still do a wrong to nature and to man.
A Government of hypocrites whose power
Extends from sea to sea, from Aristook
To Rio Grande; from Sable Cape to where
Vancouver's Inlet dents Pacific's shore;
From Northern Lakes and Mississippi's source,
To silver sands 'round Gulf of Mexico;
From wild Atlantic's to Pacific's waves,
Will not admit the wrong which we complain.

And must we wait for Justice from such men?
Must we lie dormant, like a bear encaved,
And not have power to break the galling yoke?
Must every voice be hushed at the behest
Of him elected chief of this great land?
Must we submit and, like a beaten cur,

V.

The Historian.

Still lick the hand upraised to deal the blow?
Must we consent to chain our tongues for him
Who dictates such submission to his will?
Must we be made the kidnapers of men
Who never did us wrong? and must we be
The tools of those who deal in human flesh?
And must the Northern States be made to be
The hunting-ground for slaves, and we the dogs?
Must any of their peaceful vales be made
The scene of such an outrage to our hearts?
And must their hills resound with pleading cries,
Alas! for mercy, and we heed them not?
Must many a home be rendered desolate,
And families and friends asunder torn?
From husbands, wives; fathers from children dear?
Must we see this and still uphold a law?
No! God forbid! that law must be repealed.

We hate all war, we are the friends of peace,
But if a war must come, pray let it be
A war of words, a war of pens sincere,
And in the thickest of the coming fight
You will not look in vain to see me there;
The pen has power far greater than the sword;
And yet we fear 't is feeble in our cause,
For pens have not the force of lead and steel
On beings who are so devoid of mind;
Nothing but force can have the least effect
On senseless heaps of animated clay.

Narrative.—John Brown's Speech.

If superhuman aid should be required
To rid the world of this unholy stain,
We need no angels from the heavenly sphere;
If hell is filled with angry demons damned,
Give me their aid, they have much better skill
To fight barbarians on such chosen ground;
But we ask not for supernatural power;
We have enough if we but use our own,
For GOD helps only those who help themselves.

Oh! sometimes in my wandering thoughts I wish
That I at once was Jupiter of old,
The king of gods; I'd seek for Tartarus
And make the mighty Pluto my ally;
Throughout the length and breadth of his domain,
We'd send a proclamation far and wide
For volunteers, for officers and men,
And when our ranks were thought to be complete
We'd sally forth, but not with murderous arms;
No, no! with press and pen and clarion voice,
In speech and song, oration, anthem, ode,
With banners flying in the welcome breeze,
Inscribed with "freedom to the sons of men,"
And we would wage a ceaseless war on earth,
Till not a man held property in man.
The king of the infernal regions dark
Should aid myself in ridding the fair world
Of slavery, and demons, furies, bold,
Should furnish soldiers for the grand crusade.

The Historian —Narrative.

That night, with others, I was sent to cut
The telegraphic wires; we did it sure,
And tried to join again the little band
That was to free the slaves, but were too late
To have been counted with the honored dead.
All know the history of that foolish raid,—
Its weakness, failure; it was but the throb
Of greater earthquake, rumbling far below,
That soon would shake the Nation to its base.
 We sought the rendezvous and all were gone;
Where was my girl? the horrifying thought
Half drove me mad; I could not search
Nor ask; a fugitive myself must flee,
But where? and where was she? I still ask where?
For nine years nearly have I sought in vain
North, south, east, west, and still no trace can find;
In Southern cities, palaces, I've sought,
In fields of cotton, rice and sugar cane,
Ten thousand cabins in the lonely vales,
Where backwoods planters lived secure and safe,
Where war went raging o'er their neighbors' fields,
I visited and sought, but never found.
 I learned that war meant freedom to our race,
And joined the ranks with Massachusetts' sons,
Saw battles, hardships, misery and death;
I got at length an honorable discharge
And now rejoice to know that Slavery's dead.

Narrative—Sam's Story of Sumter.

But since the close of war I 've sought again
The country over for the girl I lost,
And cannot find, and fear I never shall.
I close my weary pilgrimage of years
By visiting the grave of him who died
That I and all my race should now be free;
There I will bow and face the rising sun,
And raise my hands in praise; then each will point
To Whiteface, Marcy; they the sentries stand,
To guard the sepulcher of old John Brown.

Sam's Story of Sumter.

We have a thrilling tale to tell, and sadder song to
    sing,   [should swing;
How Sumter fell by traitor hands, by traitors that
How Major Robert Anderson, and sixty-five brave
    men,   [and then
Fought till they 'd nothing to defend except their flag,
Still fought for honor of that sheet; wherever 't was
    unfurled   [world;
That flag was hailed in every port within the Christian
Was honored and respected too, upon the land and
    sea,   [the free;
The patriot's hope, the tyrant's fear, the emblem of
The flag that ne'er was humbled yet, in three succes-
    sive wars,   [stripes and stars;
" Where red and white and blue unite," the glorious

The Historian.

But lost the fort, yes lost, and gained for us at little cost; [lost.
Our nation had been born again, that birth was Sumter
When eighty years and five around our country's brow had whirled, [rang o'er the world;
And shed their strength of manhood, and our fame
When thirty millions rose from three, a people wise and free, [thirty-three;
And thirteen weak and feeble States had grown to
When all were happy and content, with all the world at peace, [cease;
A few despotic wicked men resolve that it should
Their main pretense, the citizens of every Northern State, [trate,
Had chosen Abra'm Lincoln as their next chief magis-
And he had said in some great speech, "the day is yet to be [and half free."
When this great land will not be seen half slave-soil
'Tis South Car'lina takes the lead in these unjust desires,
Revives the spirit that imbued the ancient nullifiers,
She calls together her *wise* men and solemnly proceeds
To cut the sacred union bonds, and formally secedes.
But not content with being free from those she loaths and hates,
She woves to her unholy cause six of the cotton States,
And these combined rebellious States, traitors we all abhor |war.
Wage unprovoked and barbarous, aggressive, cruel

Sumter—The Evacuation.

'Twas Christmas night of sixty when our gallant lit-
    tle band,   [command
The gates of old Fort Moultrie left, by Anderson's
We took the boats and steered across a mile of watery
    way,   [ter lay,
The feeble moon our only guide, to where Fort Sum-
And to and fro throughout the night, we ply from
    shore to shore,   [store,
Our equipage to save from camp, and necessary
Which were secured within the walls, for at the rising
    sun,   [gun.
We beat the usual reveille, and fired the morning
December twenty-seventh came, for us a happy day,
For once again our banner we could cheerfully dis-
    play;   [brave,
A flag-staff had been planted by our soldiers bold and
The starry ensign from its truck defiantly could wave.
The men were all assembled in the midst of the parade,
And, kneeling on the sacred soil, the reverend chap-
    lain prayed   [pleading tone,
For "Peace on earth, good will to men," in earnest,
For "mercy and encouragement," before Jehovah's
    throne.   [name is praised,
Within each breast each heart responds, and as His
The brightest banner in the world by Anderson is
    raised;   [and men,
The band plays "Yankee Doodle," while the officers

The Historian—Star of the West.

Give three times three most deafening cheers, again
    and then again.   [new-made home,
But scarce two weeks have passed away within our
Ere Government a vessel sends across the ocean's
    foam,   [plies;
With reinforcements for the fort, dispatches and sup-
This vessel at the dawn of day our sentinel descries,
But just emerging from the mist, upon the ocean's
    crest,   [nest;
And steaming to her destined port—a dove unto her
When, lo! from rebel guns a shot, and ere the echo
    dies,
The starry banner to her peak as quick as lightning
    flies,   [o'er the tide
They still fire on with heavier guns, and skimming
Their dreadful missiles fly and lodge within the ves-
    sel's side;   [discern
She turns, she leaves the rebel coast, our officers
"Star of the West" a golden line on her retreating
    stern.   [men,
What were the feelings in the hearts of officers and
In Sumter at a scene like this? to see that vessel when
The stars and stripes fly up the mast, and still they
    not forbear,   [the air.
But let their shot fly thick and fast, like demons of
"Embrasures open! man the guns! put in the ten-
    inch shells!   [swells,
On Morris Island let them bear!" each manly bosom

Sumter — The Party.

To vindicate the honor of the banner of the free,
To stop the rebels' wild career nor bend the supple
    knee.   [and flies,
Ere these commands could be obeyed, the vessel turns
Our voices fail, our cheeks grow pale, and tears are
    in our eyes.   [iously await
For months our brave beleaguered band most anx-
The action of the Government to designate our fate,
For while the President pursues his vascillating
    course,
Around us rise the batteries in overwhelming force;
But still in hopes the "fourth of March" will bring a
    firmer man,   [we can;
We stint ourselves on short supplies, and do the best
It comes and goes, a month slips by, and still no fur-
    nished aid,   [and afraid;
And hearts that loyal long have been are trembling
At last our last resource is gone, surrounded by the
    tide,   [nied,
All intercouse with friends on shore prohibited, de-
And still, though starving in this fort, we raise our
    hands on high,   [die.
And swear we'll live by that old flag, or for it we will
On April eighth the President Lieutenant Talbot
    sent   [sent,
To Beauregard at Charleston and to try to gain con-
To send an unarmed vessel with provisions for the fort,

The Historian.—The Fort.

And if he'd not allow him, then, to give him this re-
  port:
" Provisions will be sent to them, and peaceably we
  trust, [must."
If not in peace they will by force, if forcibly we
He was refused, and back again to Washington he lies;
The ling'ring ray of peace for us with this refusal dies.
  Upon an artificial isle in Charleston's noble bay
Fort Sumter stands, on every side the rebel batteries
  lay, [Isle,
The nearest one on Cummings' point, a part of Morris
Is on the South, its weakest side, in distance scarce a
  mile,
No battery of simple sand, so usual now in wars,
But one of mighty strength, and clad with iron rail-
  road bars; [plight,
Fort Johnson next upon the west is now in best of
To play a most terrific part in this forthcoming fight;
Old Castle Pinckney ready too, though far to north
  of west, [test;
Is certain she can Sumter shell, and anxious for the
Fort Moultrie nearly on the east, the strongest of them
  all,
Can send a perfect hurricane of either shell or ball;
Beside upon adjacent coast that round about her lies,
A dozen smaller batteries contemptuously arise;
  These batteries are all arranged and ready to bom-
  bard

V.

Sumter.—The Attack.

Fort Sumter when the summons comes from General
    Beauregard   [yield
To Major Robert Anderson and his small force to
To these Confederate armies in the great opposing
    field.   [man's reply :
Ten thousand foes are round us, this is that brave
"My honor and my Government forbid me to comply."
'T is now the twelfth of April, eighteen hundred
    sixty-one,   [begun,
Just as the day is breaking, that the deadly work's
That Beauregard on Sumter fires his first secession
    shot,—
In all our country's history the deepest, foulest blot ;
The signal gun goes booming for the forts to open fire,
With every breaching battery, with consequences dire,
Now belching forth their fire and smoke, like light-
    ning o'er the bay,   [play ;
The red-hot shot, the bursting shells in awful grandeur
The sudden jar, the booming sound, the long-con-
    tinued roar,   [tents pour ;
Whene'er those dread Columbiads their awful con-
The quick concussion of the air, the sharper cracking
    sounds,   [sounds ;
Whene'er a rifled cannon's voice within the din re-
The low, the dull, uncertain sound, that most dis-
    tinctly tells,   [destructive shells ;
When bursts within old Sumter's walls, those most

All these combine in awful din, too horrid to rehearse,
The warfare known to savage tribes is not one whit
    the worse;   [fort,
Ten thousand men, two hundred guns against a little
And cheered by blooming Charleston belles, who
    glory in the sport.
But not until the morning's sun is far up in the sky,
Does Anderson and our brave men e'en deign to make
    reply;   [bread,
We coolly take our morning meal, exhaust our navy
And lack at that, but finish our repast with pork in-
    stead;   [given,
And now the usual morning prayer is by the chaplain
And hearts unused to fear invoke the aid of Highest
    Heaven;   [the band,
We sing a song of sacred praise, and then join with
And to their music wed the words "Columbia, Happy
    Land,"   [shame
Alas! this morning is the last, record it to the
Of Southern rebel, traitor knaves, who 've ruined our
    fair fame.
Now, calm and cool the orders come, without a vain
    parade,   [obeyed;
And just as cool, and just as calm, these orders are
The officers strip off their gold, put on their working
    suit,   [salute;
As unconcerned as though they were to fire a grand

Sumter.—Defense.

Embrasures open, guns are charged, defensive war to
   wage,
And here our history begins its saddest, darkest page.
Now on Fort Moultrie's batteries the guns are
   brought to bear, [the air;
And deadly, dev'lish missiles fly, like meteors through
On Pinckney, Johnson's, Cummings' Point, we show-
   er our fiery shells;
So careful is the aim of each, its tale of terror tells;
Twelve batteries ply their guns on us, we answer
   only four, [one more.
With men enough to man ten guns, nor ask we for
But now the common laborers, relieved of every
   fear,
Step up to Major Anderson and bravely volunteer,
They load and fire with shot and shell as ne'er was
   done before, [pour;
On Cummings' iron battery their pent-up vengeance
The young musicians follow suit, throw down their
   sounding brass,
And in their zeal, if possible, the laborers surpass;
That flattering, floating, fleeting thing has roused their
   latent ire, [tive fire
And draws from them contemptuously a most destruc-
The livelong day, the livelong night, for thirty hours
   and more, [roar.
We ply the guns' vindictive din, nor sleep amid the

The Historian.

There 's one upon the battlements, a witness in the strife, [life;
Who cannot raise a hand in aid, and yet will risk his
He views the rebel batteries, and from a dangerous spot, [or " shot !"
And when they fire he cries aloud, "look out for shell!"
The halyards of the flag are cut, the flag lies on the ground, [around,
He leaves his post amid the din of shells that burst
He takes the line between his teeth, shows strength as well as pluck, [the truck,
He climbs the slender tapering mast and reeves it in
Excels the Sergeant Jasper feat by this heroic part,
Engraving on the scroll of fame the name of Peter Hart. [us fall
We raise the flag, and still fight on, although around
The monstrous shot, and seething hot, and shells most dread of all, [raise,
Till ten o'clock the second day the cry of " fire " we
The smoke bursts from the barrack doors, the roof is in a blaze! [or fame,
We cease our fire, the buckets seize, think not of death
But shower and swash the water on the fierce devouring flame; [distress;
Half-mast, the flag is dropped, it floats, a signal of
And still these rebel chiefs fire not a shot or shell the less.

V.

Sumter—Defense.

A few go forth upon the wharf, that few are doubly
   brave, [save;
Who dip the waters of the bay our precious lives to
They 're seen, and purposely on them the iron hail is
   rained, [and gained!
All hope is gone, the flag is struck! Fort Sumter lost
Now soon arrives a boat with three commissioners
   on board, [sword.
To dictate terms to Anderson, and take his flag and
But unappalled by fear of death, regardless of his fate,
He 'll not surrender flag or fort, but will evacuate;
'T is all arranged, they wend their course across the
   silvery bay, [day.
To make report to Beauregard and wait the coming
'T is Sabbath morn, our nation's flag floats o'er the
   ruined fort;
To honor it a grand salute of fifty guns report;
The officers and men parade beneath its starry fold,
Its honor is to us as dear as either fame or gold;
The band play Yankee Doodle while with feelings
   none can tell, [Isabel;
We march with it across the wharf on board the
We leave the fort, we leave the coast, and o'er the
   briny blue, [and true,
We seek among our fellow men for those still just
Yes, "true to Country" and our homes, "for union
   hand in hand," [Native Land."
Some twenty million hearts respond, "Our God and

The Historian—Chronicle.

When I look back upon those fearful years,
  So full of woe, anxiety and dread,
And count the cost of time, of wealth and tears,
  The prison's pangs and the unnumbered dead,
My heart still shudders, it more horrid seems
Than all my wild imaginings in dreams.

The prize we fought for will affect the world,
  Not only now, but for all coming years,
In every land our flag again unfurled
  Receives the homage and the honest cheers
Of patriot men, who raise their hands to bless,
And give their thanks to GOD for our success.

Yes, war is bitter; they who live must know
  War is barbaric; if they take the sword
They take the chances of the ebb and flow
  Of that fierce tide; the semi-savage hoard
That swept o'er Britain in their fierce forays
Was much like armies in our modern days.

Sweet dove-eyed Peace, whose wings but gently fan
  The trembling nation, nervous from the strife,
Has hardly settled o'er us; may the man
  Who takes the helm be he who saved its life,—
Sweet Peace! how dear to all those words must be
To those who lost, or won, from sea to sea.

CHAPTER VI.

THE HUMORIST.

Chronicle.

My friends have ascertained that I'm a jingler,—
　That I have penned my chronicles in rhyme,—
And have requested, very strange and sing'lar,
　That I shall write a Pastoral in time
To be delivered *(*why, they're green as grass*)*,
When they return from Adirondack Pass.

Now, that will give me just about five days,
　To rake together from my various fields,
A thrifty sample from each crop that pays,—
　Some fields are barren, some have scanty yields,
And each I fear, in spite of all my care,
Will show wild mustard almost everywhere.

Of course, I know a field of corn from clover,—
　The clover grows where winter wheat grew last year,
The corn is rowed both ways the country over;
　Beside, I know a meadow from a pasture;
The pasture's grazed upon, the meadow's mowed,
But I don't know a Pastoral from an Ode.

The Humorist.

However, I will try; I 've "Rural Sports,"
   I wrote in boyhood for a monthly paper,
Beside a lot of odds and ends, all sorts
   Of farming themes. I 'll get them into shape, or,
Perhaps arrange them in some regular way,
Like flood-wood soldiers on a training day.

'T is twilight hour; on bunks, and blocks, or benches,
   My friends in silence sit, expecting fun;
I can but notice each himself entrenches
   With bags and bundles round, and every one
Is taking pains to keep his spirits down,
Like boys at circus, waiting for the clown.

The reader for the hour is our schoolmaster,—
   As full of humor as an egg of meat;
No polished writer, but a poetaster,
   Or such is all he calls himself; the treat
Has come at last that we have long desired,—
He 's kept us waiting till we all are tired.

The merry twinkle in his nut-brown eye,
   The hearty happiness that joins his laughing,
The smile that lights his face, the mimic sigh,
   Or tear, that tells you he is only chaffing,
Are indescribable in verse or prose.
But he is ready, and, of course, I close.

Panegyric on Mirth.

The only animal that laughs is man ;
 Then give him thanks who first discovered Laughter,
And bless the chap who cheers life's little span,
 No matter what his name, or race, or craft, or
Pursuit ; enjoy the boon while yet you can,
 For Sorrow 's sure to come so closely after,
The heart, hilarious in its pleasure, feels
Her scalding tear-drops trickle on its heels.

The little infant on its mother's lap,
 That squirms and squalls almost beyond enduring,
Unsatisfied with song, caress, or pap,
 Is still, thank fate within the nurse's curing ;
A shake, a hush, a hug, a kiss, a slap,
 Each turn the tune, but higher tones assuring ;
There 's still a better remedy, by half,
She tries the tickle, and she makes him laugh.

The school-boy, pouting on the dunce's block,
 And vexed with all with mirth upon their faces,
Perhaps concludes he'll give that boy a knock,
 Who 's making fun of him with queer grimaces ;
Would he be stupid, stolid as an ox,
 Were they in his, and he then in their places?
Ten minutes later, on the playing ground,
He laughs, the happiest fellow to be found.

The Humorist—Seven Ages.

A little later in the day of life,
　When "teens" are past, and age ends in t-y ty,
And looks are cast around him for a wife,
　And mind is wandering, vapory and flighty;
His keenness closed up like a pocket-knife,
　That opens brightly, when, with great delight, he
Receives acceptance as a favored lover,
You know he's happy, for he laughs all over!

And next, on life's great battle-field of toil,
　Where wealth alone is sought by honest labor,
In trade or commerce, or reluctant soil,　　　[bor,
　That yields a competence, wealth's nearest neigh-
When ease repays him for the long turmoil,
　He takes life jubilant with pipe and tabor,
And laughing lives, a merry-making roister,
As happy and contented as an oyster.

The next scene finds him in a Justice' seat,
　With heaving stomach, rounded like a barrel;
He hears with pain the tale of deep deceit,
　And tries to feel impartial in a quarrel;
But if, perchance, quaint humor gives a treat,
　He feels the keenness of wit's little carrel;
Convulsive laughter shakes his fleshy sides,
Till tears roll down his cheeks in copious tides.

Panegyric—Seven Ages

When age has thinned his shadow on the wall,
   And canes are sought to aid his failing pedal,
He seeks some old acquaintance in his stall,
   And each contrives in various ways to meddle
With other folks' affairs; they hear it all,
   And tell it, also, managing to peddle
The laughing scandal; boisterous with glee,
You hear their ha, ha! ha! and he, he! he!

Now, feebly tottering on the grave's dark brink,
   With waning intellect but faintly gleaming,
Like little sun-spots through the clouds like ink,
   In fitful flashes o'er his visage streaming;
The mind runs backward with the power to think,
   To early scenes, that seem so much like dreaming;
And recollections when he was a boy,
As death slips in, illume his face with joy.

'T is thus you see, in all life's varying years,
   Depicted in Will Shakspeare's Seven Ages,
That smiles and laughter banish briny tears,
   From want, or wealth, from simpletons or sages;
Each, in his way, complacently appears
   To pay to Momus his most welcome wages,
And takes delight in nitrous oxyde quaffing,
To gain from fate a glorious fit of laughing.
VI.

The Humorist—Varieties.

I think I wrote it twenty years ago,—
"I count that man a public benefactor,
Who makes his neighbor laugh." Is it not so?
Do you deny? Would you have me retract? Or,
Say, shall we make it classic? Friend or foe,
I'll leave unto yourselves the pleasing facture;
In your expenditures I think you "orter"
Count thirty cents in fun for every quarter.

I do endorse Democritus of old,
By counting his the only true philosophy;
All others seem so stupid, dull and cold,
They freeze the blood; the heart would surely ossify
If it were not expanded; mind would mould;
The brain laid dormant plainly soon would mossify,
And man would wither if he could not laugh,
As dry as any puff ball, sponge, or chaff.

Look back a moment to your infant days,
And think of rhymes of Mother Goose; the stories
Your mother told you, and the boyish plays
That rise in your remembrance, crowned with glo-[ries.
I willingly would wager that your Mays,
Your Marys, Helens, Sarahs and Elnoras,
Who gave you great delight and joined your laughter,
Are best remembered now—will be hereafter.

Panegyric—Shakspeare.

Deprive Will Shakspeare of his lines of mirth,
  And you would steal the oil from his machinery;
Take out the fools of high or lowly birth,
  You'd leave their castles duller than a deanery;
Remove the humor, though of little worth,
  The play's a landscape shorn of all its greenery;
If robbed of Falstaff, with his numerous sins, or
His love of sack, where is your " Wives of Windsor?"

Take any other of his plays you choose,
  That has a line of wit or humor in it;
Erase or alter, you are sure to lose,
  Though it be but a word, that very minute
The drawling lines will fairly seem to snooze;
  The song is hushed, as falls a singing linnet
Before the shot of some inhuman fowler;
So would he suffer from a filching prowler.

The man who steals the greenback from my fob,
  Has got a piece of promising pretty paper;
I earn another by some extra job,—
  By sitting later at the midnight taper;
But he who steals my joke contrives to rob
  My dearest treasure,—'t is a dirty caper,—
'T is worse than robbing, it exceeds manslaughter,
He steals the soul of Mirth; give him no quarter.
VI.

The Humorist—Comic Poets.

O, Comic Poets! you who sweetly wrote
    The quaint conceits, the syllabub of humor,
The sparkling wit, of which we love to quote,
    The broad burlesque, or tender, tickling tumor;
Those pleasing pleasantries on which we dote,
    The satire keen of those well known to rumor;
Your lines will stand the test of petty malice,
They're pictures painted in a prince's palace.

No doubt the poetry of ancient times,
    Contains some gems of mirth-provoking fancy;
But those old poets were not cramped with rhymes,
    Nor were they troubled with a weak Miss Nancy,
Who criticised their lines, and held as crimes
    The slightest deviation in the prance he
Put Pegasus upon, toward Parnassus,
And, consequently, they may all surpass us.

I do n't read Latin, or attempt the Greek,
    Nor ride a Pegasus, or e'en a pony,
Nor bathe in Helicon, or Muses seek,
    Nor mix my verses in a macaroni;
I try in my vernacular to speak,
    Although my stream of talk is rather stony;
'T is better far than being smooth and vapid,—
What is a river worth without a rapid?

Panegyric—Old Poets.

I have no knowledge of those Grecian bards,
   Excepting Pope's translation of old Homer.
They've never sent their photographic cards
   To my address, and as I am no roamer
I ne'er shall know them, for the safety guards
   So thick are 'round each musty covered tome, or
The tedious distance I should have to travel,
Prevents our meeting;—I must bind my gavel.

But why should we go back a thousand years,
   To seek for fun from those old poetasters,
When since their days occasionally appears
   The brilliant lights of our old English masters,
Who woke the world with mirth till crystal tears
   Suffused the cheek, like sorrowful disasters;
Earth fairly trembled with the sides then shaking,
And monks and nuns supposed the world was quaking.

But not to poets is all wit confined;
   There may be mirth in those who write prosaic;
Whose spotted pages tempt the jocund mind
   With motley medley beautifully mosaic;
Whose flash of fancy is so well refined,
   You cannot tell the movement from Alcaic;
Or many others of those Grecian measures
That classic scholars hold among their treasures.

The Humorist.—Parodies.

And writers, also, of unvarnished prose,
    Have scattered broadcast mirth and witticism
With such profusion, no young author knows
    But that he's liable to criticism;
He may be treading on his neighbor's toes,—
    In making fun may raise a bit of schism;
And has been stealing, though he does not know it;—
When e'er you think I steal put marks to show it.

The man who has no mirth within his heart,
    Who is not moved with Wit's provoking shaft, or
Who feels no happier when the comic part
    Of human nature's uppermost, is daft, or
Else he is fit to take the traitor's part,
    And play the murderer to healthy laughter,
Or rob a grave-yard; hold! the measure breaks here,
To say that this is parodied from Shakspeare.

I would not count him as my nearest friend,
    Though clad in broadcloth of the finest quality,
With polished boots upon his pedaled end,
    If he should deem my funny-dotes frivolity;
Nor would I seek him, though he'd cash to lend,
    Unless he'd join my joke with joyful jollity;
Your trust in me, I fear, is now some shaken;
That is not Cowper, you are quite mistaken.

Panegyric—Wits.

I wish I 'd time to mention half the wits
  Now dead, that only lived that they might tickle us ;
Whose fancy fairly every folly fits,
  From broad burlesque to whimsical ridiculous ;
The subtle satire or ironic hits
  With which in some way they contrived to pickle us,
Poor erring mortals ; well, I 'll not aspire,
Their names would stretch like telegraphic wire.

Oh, were I able (it is plain I 'm not)
  I 'd tribute pay to those I often sigh for ;
The charming Neal, poor Poe, and quaint " Bedott,"
  And " Ward" and " Phœnix," oh ! what did they die for?
Though missed, they cannot surely be forgot,—
  (We weave the laurel wreath around each cipher;)
And though their thoughts awoke our hearts in gladness,
We 'll speak their names with reverence and sadness.

I count each witty writer in the land,
  Each living humorist, a worthy brother ;
To each, if present, I 'd extend the hand
  With hearty welcome ; hold ! perhaps my mother
Might think her progeny like grains of sand
  Upon a beach, no matter ; with none other
Would I e'er mix, and follow inclination,
Save those whose minds excite my cachination.
  VI.

But let me lay the covers for my friends,
    And let me set them at my supper table,
Yourself and I shall occupy the ends,
    The others I 'll arrange as I am able.
As brilliant color to enjoyment tends,
    None shall appear in garments sad or sable,
And our repast, though simple, (what 's the odds?)
Shall be a banquet worthy of the gods.

First on my right is Hosea Bigelow,
    Old Mrs. Partington, and then Mace Sloper.
Upon my left is Fanny Fern, below
    Comes Holmes, and next Gail Hamilton, no moper;
Now on your right, Q. K. Philander Doe—
    With Jenny June and Kerr, no interloper;
Then on your left, Ik Marvel with his garland,
And next Josh Billings, after, Marion Harland.

Upon my right, next, spicy Edmund Kirke,
    With Florence Percy, and the genial Knicker'—
Then on my left Jeems Pipes, with lots of work
    For Mary Clavers, Sparrowgrass, that brick, or
Now on your right, Tim Titcomb, spruce as clerk,
    Beside the Reverend Nasby, full of liquor;
Then, on your left is Pepper, with his crony
The gentle youth, the gushing McArone.

Panegyric—The Supper.

For our repast we have but griddle cakes,
   With golden rolls, and amber-colored syrup;
You know precisely how such feeding makes
   A miscellaneous company so chirrup;
They all ride hobbies, and each rider takes
   The pains to show his foot is in the stirrup;
Especially if they should chance to be
Exhilarated by my "Smartweed Tea."

The raising power within my cakes is Wit,
   The flour, the very finest Flower of Humor;
The butter, made of Cream of Jokes, and it
   Was churned by laughing, Flora its perfumer;
The sweetest lines by loving poet writ,
   The sap, and boiled by night's serene illumer
This is the food I offer to each friend;
If he don't like it he need not attend.

Let knives and forks make music on each plate,
   Till we have cleaned the oft replenished platter,
And frightened cook at last compelled to state
   That she has not another drop of batter;
Let "cups to cheer, but not inebriate,"
   Go circling 'round with less important matter,
And dished in rare and intellectual olla,
Sal Atticum ab ova ad mala.

The Humorist—Invocation.

I feel I should a touching tribute pay
   To circus clowns, who first raised my hilarity;
And next, the better acted comic play,
   Or puzzling pantomime, the pleasing rarity;
The punch and judy of a " Training Day,"
   And ventriloquial efforts, sounding parrotty;
But last, and best, and cheapest fun on earth,—
The Negro Minstrel's cataract of mirth.

Long life to Laughter! May the merry god
   With cherry cheeks, look slily o'er my shoulder,
And touch my nose; if I'm inclined to nod,
   Or grow prosaic, he may still be bolder,
And stuff my ears with anything that's odd,
   Till I'm too full of Mirth to longer hold her.
I take it Mirth's a female with long wings,
Because prolific, and of flying things.

Relentless Death, if you must snatch the clay
   That holds these jewels, like a precious casket,
For mortals' sake, put off the fatal day
   Till more are born; dim in the future mask it;
A million souls petitioning, will pray
   In deep solicitude, and humbly ask it, [portal,
That when you take them through your darkened
You'll leave their wit to some succeeding mortal.

Putting on Airs.

'T is a curious fact in all human affairs,
That mankind will in someway be putting on airs.
There is hardly a man that 's content to appear
To the eyes of the world in his natural gear.
From the President down to the humblest schoolmaster,
From the College Professor to young poetaster,
From the Judge on the bench to the honest shoemaker,
From the doctor at birth to polite undertaker,
From the richest to poorest, from the highest to lowest,
From the oldest to youngest, from the fastest to slowest,
Yes, in every condition I safely can name,
There are some who make fools of themselves, to their shame.

Oft the rich ape the poor, and the poor ape the wealthy;
Oft the well think they 're sick, and the sick think they 're healthy; [scholars,
Oft the learned talk like dunces, and dunces like
Often beggars get pence that are given for dollars,
You can oft get advice that is very well meant, [sent;
That would not be received at the source whence 't was
Here a short man invariably wears a tall hat,
And a tall one, contrariwise, one that is flat;
Here a man that 's robust will be pinched in the waist,
And another that 's thin will be padded in taste;
All of which you must take with a small grain of salt,
For there 's no man so poor that he cannot find fault.

The Humorist—The Women.

Now if this was confined to the men folks alone,
I 'd feel perfectly safe in the picking this bone;
But the women are equally guilty with men,
Though it may not be fair to attack them with pen,
For the weapon they parry and thrust with, the tongue,
Is so easily managed by old ones or young,—
Is so mild, is so sweet, is so sharp, is so keen,
It allures, it betrays, it enslaves with its sheen,
'T is as light as the thistle down floating in ether,
And as sharp as the thistle you tread on the heather,
And for fear the gay girls may attack me in masses,
While I laugh at their follies, I 'll take them in
   classes.

There is many a homely one plays she is pretty,
There is many a dull one pretends to be witty,
There is often a handsome one says she is plain,
And as often a modest one tries to be vain ;
Oft an ignorant one will assume to be wise,
And the gayest in heart will act prim and precise ;
When their words are the warmest their hearts are at
   zero,   [Nero ;
When they 're touchingly tender they 're cruel as
If they treat you with coldness they 're sure to accept
   you,   [you ;
If they smile at your offer they 're sure to reject
And it all may be fair with the fair, in affairs
Of this kind, for they always are putting on airs.

Putting on Airs—The President.

There is one who I venture to wager a bowl on,
Who believes he 's the ancient philosopher Solon ;
He would have us admit transmigration of souls,
The resemblance between them is wide as the poles.
As a lunatic Solon went spouting his verses,
So a lunatic Blank, his loose verbiage rehearses,
As a law-giver, Solon was thought to be wise,
But 't is otherwise only with Blank, if he tries ;
Number one, as we know, well united a nation,
Number two would divide us with long agitation.
Number one left his country to travel ten years,
If this Blank would resemble him there, we 'd give
    cheers.

Mister Blank boasts his birth from the lowest of strata,
And can figure his progress from simplest of data ;
But the data he uses are false, for it seems
'T is the filth of the country that floats on the streams,
And the worst of creation, the scum of mankind,
Can oft float into office, the highest we find.
He 's so fuddled with fame, and so terribly mixed, he
Oft presumes to know more than the whole of the
    sixty
Who this versatile verdant's voluminous vetoes
Have oft brushed, as we brush away flies and mos-
    quitoes.
He is putting on airs, and it may be he feels
Like a Cæsar with Senate *that barks* at his heels.

The Humorist—The Cabinet.

Mister Seward's ambition than race horse is faster,
He desires to die richer than John Jacob Astor,
Whom, mayhap, you have heard of; he died long ago,
And had made a small fortune in peltry, you know.
So our Seward, as Steward, concluded to buy
All our furs up at wholesale, and keep a supply,
And will retail them out to the girls; but the charm
Of the purchase to him, is the breadth of his farm,
For our States are increasing so fast, that he feels
He is perfectly safe in supplying them seals.
As we've been in the tide of hot water at flood,
He may think it an ice way to cool off our blood.

Mister Stanton, of Washington long time a resident,
Has conceived the idea that he is the President,
And His Accidency, he whose brain is so addle,
In the fear he may be such, has bid him skedaddle;
But young Edwin declares there's a fact he don't
    think on,—
He was placed in the chair by the late Mister Lincoln,
And he will not vacate it in any event,
Unless Andy insists and the Senate consent;
Though I wish Mr. Stanton were chief of the nation,
In the place of that wickedest man in creation,
I much fear in the end he'll be kicked down the stairs,
Not because he is wrong, but, for putting on airs.

Putting on Airs—The Cabinet.

Mister Stanberry, gracious! was Boswell more handy
To his Johnson than this one is to his old Andy?
Can't he write "an opinion as is an opinion,"
As a Cuttle would say of his power and dominion?
Can't he echo the words of his garrulous master,
Like the raven of Rudge,—even thicker and faster?
He is learned in the law, for a stripling quite plucky,
And can quote laws quite obsolete, e'en in Kentucky.
He's so bright there is nothing on earth can deceive him,—
What a pity the Senate will never believe him!
Does he sell at "Mock Auction?" they don't take his wares,
And they treat him as though he were putting on airs.

I could easily treat the whole Cabinet thus,
And could claim them all candidates in for the muss.
But their chances, of course, are decidedly slim,
When compared with Judge Chase's, (I must not miss him);
He has got a soft thing that will last him for life,
And why he should take chances in partisan strife,
Is a query to me. Tell me, why should he seek
For a favor from foes? Is he foolish, or weak?
When the Democrats meet in quadrennial convention
He will not get a prize, or an " honorable mention,"
As the judges would say at Mechanical Fairs,
And 'tis merely because he is putting on airs.

The Humorist—The Senate.

In the Senate I'm sure there's a dozen, at least,
Who would like to have " cards to admit " to the feast.
Some are nervously bold, some are nervelessly weak;
Some can wearily write, and some cunningly speak.
They pretend they're not candidates,—" I'm no such
    fool," [school,
Say they all, but they are; since they first went to
And their schoolmistress said, as they went to their
    plays,
That perhaps they'd be Presidents one of these days,
If they did not chop cherry trees, did not tell lies;
(How their little hearts beat; how they opened their
    eyes);
And from that very day, why, the chiefest of cares
Has for them been the White House; they're putting
    on airs.

I must single out one, though, in fact, I'm afraid
He was never found wanting, and that is Ben Wade.
He may write to his friends, or his foes, if he chooses,
He will take what he gets, as he never refuses;
And why should he? if people will vote for old Ben,
They've a right to, and he is a king among men.
But he must not indite us another long letter, [better,
To announce " he don't want it;" he knows we know
But, of course, he's not got e'en the ghost of a chance
On the course which each candidate usually grants.
He'll withdraw in the favor of one, when he dares
To be honest; but now, he is putting on airs.

Putting on Airs—The House.

In the lower House, likewise, are some, without doubt,
Who aspire to be first, knowing what they're about,
And in pulling the wires, if they cannot be first,
Will assume to predict that the party will burst;
If they can't have the place number two on the ticket,
They will bolt from the party, then turn 'round and lick it;
If they can't have a place in the Cabinet, sure,
Then our nation's a humbug, and cannot endure;
With a medium intellect, motives most sinister, [ter,
They presume they deserve to be some foreign minis-
But, astonished, the multitude stupidly stares,
To observe them so blusteringly putting on airs.

There is Colfax, he's clever,—a printer by trade,
And, of course, knows how men have by printing been made;
Printer's ink is so cheap, and so smooth tells a story,
You can cover a rogue in a minute with glory.
He has got the advantage of most politicians,
He can lecture on temperance, labor and missions;
He can spout for the party and write for the Union,
He can travel on Sunday, or go to communion;
He can figure and calculate, guess, and has reckoned
If he cannot be first, he perhaps will be the second.
He would take it, of course, and would whistle, "who cares?"
But it all would be his way of putting on airs.
VI.

The Humorist—The Governors.

Full a hundred and sixty odd Governors, surely,
Would each like to be President ; motives so purely
Patriotic as theirs, should receive some attention,
But ungrateful Republics, and party dissension
Keep them out in the cold; imitating one, Jackson,
They retire to a farm, and to office turn backs on,
Oft pretending they 're tired of the arduous station,
And the scramble for office, or party dictation—
They 've been cloyed with emoluments, fretted with toil,
And can only take pleasure in tilling the soil,
Or as Presidents acting at Dairymen's Fairs,　[airs.
But you need not believe them ; they 're putting on

I 'll select one at random, no dullard or dreamer,
Who pretends he 's no candidate ; he is a seemer ;
He has written long letters to numerous friends,
To assure them through life he now only intends
To be simply a farmer, the bone of the nation,
Not a bone of contention to get nomination ;　[less,
But this " Saymore " will say more and have it mean
Than a clown in a circus, I 'm free to confess,
And this Seymour will see more (Horatio remember,)
Red Republican votes on the fifth of November
Than were ever before ; don't decide till he swears
He will never accept it : he 's putting on airs.

Putting on Airs—The Generals.

As the last Army Register lately revealed,
We have fifty full Generals fresh from the field,
And if this were too little to heighten our fears,
There are ninety-nine hundred and nine Brigadiers.
Who desire to be President; seeming propriety—
Might, perhaps, make them such, of a little society
That is formed the great temperance cause to promote,
Then the good might go up, not the bad down the throat.
They have been in all battles on land and on sea,
From the flight at Bull Run to surrender of Lee,
And each thinks with his claim not another compares,
He is deeply in earnest, but puttings on airs.

Since it would not be fair to select, save their chief,
To illustrate my point I'll be decent and brief;
Politicians may urge him, e'en women beseech,
They cannot get a letter or a part of a speech.
He can calculate chances, if not he's a fool
That's determined to win and keep perfectly cool.
He has planned his great battle, has counted his forces,
He has got his reserves of provisions and horses,
The munitions of war and the choice of position,
And the pluck for a backing of noble ambition,
There is no smoke about him, excepting cig-*airs*,
He'll accept it; Ulysses is putting on airs.

The Humorist—Everybody.

None are putting on airs any worse than our preachers
Worthy Cheevers and Chapins, or Bellows and Beech-
    ers;   [ior,
They oft make themselves judges of christian behav-
Arrogating the office of Maker, or Savior.

    Our physicians, likewise, and no matter what 'pathy,
Will abuse one another, get foolish and wrathy,
And expect in another what they themselves lack,
Saying, "Our system's science; all others are quack,"

    And our lawyers, especially young ones, we know
Are so much like young cocks we expect them to
    crow;
But they put on such airs in their eloquent fury,
You'd suppose them a trio,—judge, client and jury.

There are Editors, also, who, acting as media,
Through which all knowledge comes, or an encyclo-
    pedia,   [least,
Will assume to know more of that thing they know
Than an ignorant, green, astrological priest.

    I could write thus a week on a theme so prolific,
And become quite offensive; I should be pacific;
So I'll close up my subject, and tie up my rhyme,
Not for lack of rich matter, but simply of time.
For we authors as well as all other professions, [sions,
Occupations and trades, must e'en make our conces-
We acknowledge with candor, without splitting hairs,
We are almost continually Putting on Airs.

Boarding Around.

Let me tell you old stories of Josh U. A. Smith,
    Quite a rhyming, a roving and rollicking blade,—
A live Yankee by birth, not a mythical myth,
    A half-poet, a wit, and a teacher by trade.
He once taught a large school in the old town of
    Tully,   [riches,
Where the people are great, if you speak of their
But the pupils they sent were so deucedly dull, he
    Often gave them a whipping, a remedy which is
Quite a sure panacea for everything evil,
Not excepting a woman, a boy, or the de-vil.
But of this never mind; to my tale more profound
Of his trials and troubles in boarding around.

On his first day in school, when the clock had struck
    four,
    He was terribly hungry, for dinner he'd none;
There his pupils sat anxiously eyeing the door,
    With a wonder why 't was that they could not be
    gone;
But to go without supper he could not afford,
    To say nothing of lodging upon the cold ground,
He had "thirteen a month" and, exclusive of board,
    Which of course he must gather in roaming around,
He commenced to inquire of the pupils before him,
    If they knew that their parents expected to see him?
If the bed had been aired where they purposed to
    store him?

VI.

The Humorist.

If their mothers were ready to toast or to tea him?
But there was not a pupil within the whole school,
   Who had parents all ready to lodge or to feed him.
So he feelingly told them he 'd made it a rule, [him;
   Not to stay but a day where the folks did not heed
"There's a hotel," said he, "in the village near by,
   Where the landlord is kind, and his daughter is waiter,—
I will go there and board till the people here try
   To supply me with lodging, some meat and *pertater*."
He had not been an hour in the tavern, I guess,
   Ere a half dozen farmers drove up at the door,
For each one had concluded he 'd be "in a mess,"
   If they let him board there and they footed the score.
Why, their bills would be higher, and that would not do,   [such wages;
   They had promised too much when they offered
But to pay for his board, and at tavern rates, too,
   They would surely be crazy and ready for cages;
So then, this trustee urged him, and that trustee coaxed him,
   And this old farmer flattered, and that farmer teased,
Till with teasing and coaxing, and urging, they hoaxed him,
   And at last he went home with the first of trustees.

Mister Smith did n't do just ezackly z'd orter,
For he orter a-staid there and courted the dorter,

Boarding Around.

Since the fellow she wed in a year after that,
Got as much as ten thousand,—that's cutting it fat,—
Though he might have lost school, aye, and even his breeches,
He'd have had an equivalent—wife, home, and riches.

Everything now went nice, for the programme was altered,
   Mister Smith was invited to tea, and was toasted,
He was flattered, and fed, for then nobody faltered,
   When their turn came to board him, and some of them boasted,
Or quite often asserted in language the strongest,
   That of all in the district they'd board him the longest;
But the quarrels the oftenest engaged in, the worst
To decide who'd accommodate Mister Smith first.
But he kept his own time to the smallest iota,
And he gave them, he says, each their regular quota;
But to stop all their fights and attendant vexation,
He commenced to go 'round, and in reg'lar rotation;
When the lofty, the lowly, the poor and the rich,
Must be ready to take him, and no matter which.

This had been going on for a fortnight or so
   Very nicely indeed, as there was not a lack
Of attention from every one, friend or a foe,
   Until suddenly he was switched off from the track.

VI.

The Humorist.

Master Jones made a signal, he wanted to speak, [ed,
  The permission, of course, was most readily grant-
For the teacher desired to know just what he wanted.
" Mother wants you to board, sir, at our house next
    week ;"
At the time he was boarding with old Mr. Boggs,
Who had two lovely daughters, he was n't a dunce,
  So he asked an excuse. " Waal, we 're gwaan to
    kill hogs,
And my ma wants her dirty work all done to once !"
Who does not know a man who is wealthy but stingy,
  One who might live at ease, but invariably delves?
He 's the type of a class who go threadbare and dingy,
  They are little enough to take care of themselves.
Deacon Jones's own class; well, he went there to
    board, [twenty,
Where the hogs had been killed, either eighteen or
And to lose a half pound they could not well afford,
  For the plucks on the cherry trees hung in great
    plenty.
He had liver for breakfast, and dinner, and supper,
  Ah! in fact you may say that he lived upon liver ;
If I had but the genius of Martin F. Tupper,
  I would write here some words that would make
    your heart shiver ;
But I own I can't do it; I 'm not worth a—clam
To eat bacon, pork, spare-rib, pig, shoulder, or ham ;

Boarding Around.

And then, as for my writing on subjects like these,
They 're so greasy I usually pass them with ease.

Well, he boarded three weeks with this old Deacon Jones,
And he lived upon liver the whole of the time,
Till he looked more like liver on muscles and bones,
Than he did like a man full of nonsense and rhyme.
At the very last meal he was going to eat,
He concluded to live upon liver no more,
But he took at the table as usual his seat,
With one eye on his hat and one eye on the door.
Deacon Jones asked a grace of the Heavenly Giver,
And then asked Mister Smith to take some of the liver.
But he firmly refused, in the softest of tones;
" I 'm afraid you do n't like it," said old Mistress Jones.
"Yes I do," said our hero, "when a poor fellow feels
Just exactly right for it, good liver is good,
And I think I should like it for sixty odd meals,
But for regular diet I do n't think I should!"

The next man in rotation was Hans Christian Schneider, [hawker;
Whose cognomen proclaimed him an ancient Mo-
The long evening passed quickly, he 'd apples and cider,
And his frow was a pleasant and excellent talker.
When the ancient Dutch clock on the bracket struck nine,

The Humorist.

And the children commenced to skedaddle for bed,
Though to follow, the teacher seemed not to incline,
Many hints were so broad, the " good nights" were
    soon said.   [did
The front chamber was large, and the furniture splen-
With the feather beds piled up as high as the chin,
When his evening devotions were happily ended,
    Then the light was soon out, and our hero soon in.
But the bed was deceptive; all night long he tumbled,
    There was something beneath him confoundedly
        hard;   [and grumbled,
So he kicked, threshed, and rolled, foamed fretted
    But could not change his spots any more than a pard.
On the back side, the fore side, the foot or the head,
    Each one had the same mountain of lead in the center
That persistingly crowded him out of the bed,
    That he was most unceasingly trying to enter.
But the long wished for morning came peeping at last,
    As it broke through the window panes frosted with
        amber,
'T was a paradise gained from the hades he'd passed,
    A procrustean bed, an inquisitor's chamber.
He was speedily dressed and for breakfast was ready;
    But concluded to learn what annoyed him all night,
So he stripped off the clothes; under one feather bed
    he
    Soon discovered the cause—a ridiculous sight.

Boarding Around.

Rolled in woolen sheets, petticoats, drawers and
   stockings,
Was the bundle of evil that tortured his ease;
Curiosity triumphed! How horribly shocking!
'T was a twelve-quart tin pan of fermenting Dutch
   cheese!

He commenced on the next week with DonaldMc Vey,
   Who was proud of his birth-place, the Emerald Isle,
And was ever bepraising that "jim of the saa,"
   In a language that often would cause you to smile.
He revered and respected the teacher's vocation,
   With obsequiousness honest, but almost digusting;
He was ready, no doubt, to pay due adoration,
   If the custom required it, not even mistrusting
That himself and the teacher were every way equal,
And the way McVey showed it you'll see in the sequel.
   For five days Smith had taken his meals all alone,
In the cosiest part of the room, from a stand,
   Not permitted to join them around the hearth-stone
At their family meal, as a family band;   [together,
   And he wondered why 't was they could not eat
When in everything else all seemed equal and free;
   "So," says he, "I will try him and ascertain
      whether
This McVey is too proud, or too modest;" said he,
" Now, McVey, will you honestly tell what you think ;
Say, for instance, if I should invite you to drink,

And we drank, do you think we 'd be equal ? now say."
"Ah ! indade, an' we would, sir," said Donald McVey.
" Well, again, at the church, either your own or mine,
We 're together partaking the bread and the wine ;
Would you think we were equal ? now tell me, I pray."
"An' av coorse we would be, sir," said Donald McVey.
" Well, suppose 'tis election, while casting our votes,
Or are blowing for candidates, splitting our throats ;
Are we equal, no matter who carries the day ?"
"Faith, you know that we are, sir," said Donald McVey.
"Once again, in the jury box, trying a cause,
In deciding disputes or the breaking of laws ;
With the fine education you know I possess,
While the little you have does not count you the less,
You remain yet my equal, and draw the same pay."
" Be the powers, yer right, sir," said Donald McVey.
" Please imagine our country is lacking of men,
And involved in a quarrel ; we equal are then ;
If we 're drafted we furnish a 'sub.' or go, eh ?
" Ye 're sound on the gander," said Donald McVey.
" Well, suppose we should go, and, by bad luck, are taken
By the foe, and compelled to eat hoecake and bacon.
They would treat us precisely alike, wouldn't they ?"
"I persoome that they would, sir," said Donald McVey.
" Then, in every condition we think of in life,
Either social, religious, in peace or in strife,

Boarding Around.

"We are every way equal ; please tell without babel
Why it is that you'll not let me dine at your table."
" Wait a bit, Misther Smith, it is joking ye a-are,
And to gammon me now izn't dacent or fair ;
As a taacher yer more than my aqual, indade,
And somehow I must show my respect for the thrade."
As the next week brought Christmas, the teacher was merry,
For his host was a native of Albion's hills,
Who rejoiced in the name of Pitt Wellington Perry ;
He had plenty of flesh, with but few of its ills ;
He had cheeks somewhat rosy, he dearly loved h-ale,
'E 'd an h-appetite greedy, to which he could pander,
All his visions of viands grew feeble and pale, [der.
As he thought of his Christmas and fat roasted gan-
Well, the supper he longed for was "A. number one,"
The old gander was roasted and turned to a T ;
Mistress P. was in luck, everything was well done,
And the happiest mortal P. W. P.,
For he ate, drank, and stuffed till beginning to dander,
He first toasted Buchanan, the Queen, then the gander.
Sadly mixed with a bacchanal song he was roaring,
Went to floor, went to sleep, and he soon went to snoring.
Now, this gander was large, and the family small,
And the fowl was no more than a quarter used up ;
Mister Smith soon found out he must conquer it all,

The Humorist.

For on it he must breakfast, must dine, and must sup.
I have mentioned for supper 'twas fat gander roasted,
For his breakfast 'twas fat gander buttered and toasted,
For his dinner some slices were placed in his basket,
For his supper again, although he did not ask it.
For his breakfast sometimes it was old gander broiled,
For his supper occasionally tough gander boiled;
For his dinner each day it was blue gander cold,
Till some twenty-one meals had reluctantly rolled;
He still lived upon gander; no soul in the house
Ever ate of that gander, not even a mouse.
Though the fowls were quite plenty, by no means were dear,
Perry would not indulge more than once in a year;
'T was a viand, a tid-bit, a luxury rare,
Much too good for all men but a teacher to share.

Honest poverty is no disgrace that is certain, [scorn,
And the man is a wretch who would treat it with
But sometimes it is covered with pride's flimsy curtain,
That is just as transparent as an old powder-horn.
Then I think, and what other folks think is no matter,
'T is for me a legitimate subject for satire.
In the cities we know many people are poor,
And 't is sometimes the case, the poorer the prouder,
They who wish to show off, where the plate on the door [louder.
Is much larger and brighter, where hall-bell rings

Boarding Around.

They who give the most parties and send the most presents, [dresses,
Where their girls' are arrayed in the costliest
With their trails that are long as the tails of some pheasants,
And so lavish of jewelry, feathers and tresses;
To keep up this deception and cling to the fashion,
Will half-starve their poor bodies to make a great show,
Like a runaway steed they impetuously dash on
Till they're utterly wrecked or have caught a rich beau.
In a small country ville 't is exactly the same,
They who least can afford it will try to look wealthy,
And they talk of poor people in language of shame,
Little thinking they're equally happy if healthy
And unheeding the truth in this ancient remark
That " the finest of timber has roughest of bark.

Josh U. A. went to board with such people as those
I have tried to describe; they were poor, but were proud; [nose,
If their neighbors were poorer they turned up their
And then talked of their poverty lengthy and loud;
But the supper was splendid, the plated cake basket
Was so passed Mr. Smith was obliged to admire it,
But the bread was so stale they determined to mask it
With nice honey, though surely he did not desire it,

The Humorist.

They had elegant china; the spoons and the forks
  Looked like silver, and pure as the heart of their daughter,
While the tea, a decoction of dry chips and corks,
  Was so pure it did not even color the water.
After supper was done came long hours of scandal,
  Till our hero concluded he'd better retire;
He was shown to his room with a tallow dip candle,
  That had none of the furniture he might desire;
But his dreams were all pleasant; the daylight was breaking,
  Jackson Frost on the panes had made fanciful trees,
Please imagine his feelings and horror on waking,
  When he hears a boy calling in accents like these:
"Please get up! Mister Smith, please get up, if you're able,   [table."
For my ma wants that clean sheet to spread on the
The old District Smith taught in embraced a small village
  Of the handsomest kind, for around every dwelling
Were nice gardens for fine horticultural tillage;
  But how many exactly 't is not easy telling;
There were shops for the varied mechanical trades,
  An old Grist Mill, I think, and a Church with a steeple,
And another without, so of different grades
  In the scale of religion were most of the people.

Boarding Around.

There were some who were better, of course, than
  their neighbors,
And they walked with an aristocratical stride;
There are some who despise any person that labors,
Go in which way you will, but it can't be denied
As a nation we hate this cod-fish aristocracy,
We can't kneel to a fellow who merely has money,
Wealthy birth does not count in our Yankee democ-
  racy,
We as soon pay respect to a man who writes funny.
Mister Smith composed verse, wore his shirt *a la*
  Byron, [story,
He could sing a good song and could tell a good
And if praise had been wealth he could each night
  retire on
A small fortune, and live upon honor and glory.
Everybody liked Josh; yes, and everyone praised him,
Had he been a bit vain it would surely have crazed
  him.

Widow Blake kept a boarding-house down by the
  church; [married,
She was "fat, fair and forty," had wished to get
And she once "set her cap" for the old teacher, Birch,
Who was sixty-five certain; she worried and harried
The old gentleman so that he gave up the school,
Left the country,—and now, as experience taught
  her

The Humorist.

That she hardly could hope to obtain an old fool,
  She must soon find a young one to marry her daughter.
So she baited her hooks for all species of fish,
Though they nibbled, they none of them bit to wish wish,
Till she fairly despaired of e'er getting a lover.
Mister Smith came to board and she reveled in clover.

Her most dutiful daughter, the shy Imogene,
Was decidedly handsome, her age just nineteen;
A much lovelier lass very seldom is seen,
With so comely a form and so noble a mien,
That was brilliant in joy, and in sadness serene.
Oh, the light of her soul was her hazel-brown een,
Just like peaches her cheeks, none too plump or too lean, [between
Then her teeth were like pearls, you could see them
Her twin lips red as flowers of the Chilian bean;
From her brow like a snow bank, as cold and as clean,
Auburn hair flowing free only served as a screen
To protect her white neck from the sun's searching sheen. [green,
As she tripped through the garden or danced on the
In an easy and graceful poetic careen,
She betrayed feet and ankles you could not demean,
And resembled a sylph or a fairy I ween,
Superadding a beauty to beautiful scene,
Such as novelists make of a countess or queen.

Boarding Around.

All her knowledge of love she had gained from romances,
Where the hero's fine steed most invariably prances,
And his armor is bright, and his long flashing lances
Prove him victor at once in the tournament's chances,
Where the prize cannot surely increase his finances.
Knights and dames crowd around as he gaily advances,
To be crowned with the ivy, the laurel and pansies
By the village's belle, queen of Mary's and Nancy's.
As she blushingly knights him he happily fancies
She is dying to whirl in the mazes of dances,
Where the music with beauty the senses entrances,
And the beauty is native, the music from Frances is,
And the quivering moonbeams the transport enhances;
Where a sigh tells a tale, and an amorous glance is
Declaration enough for the too willing Frances, [is
For the heart that so strangely now flutters and pants,
But the prize he is seeking, she tremblingly grants his
Request to become his dear " Duchess of Ances."

Then a marriage takes place and the honeymoon over,
And she happily dreams she is living in clover.
But a year rolls around, she's a chance to discover
That the clouds that so brilliantly floated above her,
Now around her all darkly and gloomily hover;
For the Knight that she wed was a villainous rover,
Emigrating at Calais and landing at Dover,
Illegitimate son of illiterate drover,

The Humorist

And the squire of a traveling, peddling glover,
Who deserted her when he no longer could cover
His base perfidy more, and determined to prove her
As unfaithful to him ; but as true as a dove, or [her,
As an infant she proved ; he could leave but not love
And retained what she could not recover in trover.
Yes, the heart that was pure as an innocent plover,
So confidingly loving, so trusting, moreover,
That she gave to the treacherous, recreant lover,
Has been robbed of its jewel, the commonest stover,
Now lies broken and bleeding and cannot recover,
Neither can it be patched by a Baker and Grover.

Now this widow endeavored by cunningest art
   To obtain for her daughter the hand of our hero,
But he made her believe that his obdurate heart
   Had gone down in the cold ten degrees below zero,
As the boarders each night would in silence retire,
   Leaving Smith and the widow and Imogene sparking
They would cosily chat by the sitting-room fire,
   Little thinking, of course, there was any one larking.
Then the widow wooed Smith, who was wooing the daughter,
Who each night fell asleep by his side on the sofa,
Till a month had rolled round, either longer or shorter,
And as neither had gained of the other a trophy,

Mistress Blake thought of course he would love
  Imogene,   [love him;
Mister Smith thought it strange Imogene could not
Imogene thought our hero decidedly "green"
To admire a poor girl; there were many above him
In their wealth who would gladly have jumped at the
  offer
Of his heart and his hand, but it was not romantic
For the man to love her with no dimes in her coffer,
And she came very nearly to driving him frantic;
All his timid advances she met with such boldness,
  That he was completely disarmed in a trice,   [ness
All his warm declarations she heard with such cold-
  That she fastened his tongue like a fish in the ice.
But the heart that was in him by no means was *froze*
  And he wrote her love billets and sent them by
    mail,
In the sweetest of verses, when beaten in prose,
  But the Muse gained him naught, he was likely to
    fail.

He confessed to the widow he loved Imogene,
  And implored her and begged her to aid him to win
    her,
" Why I've known it," said she, " you are looking so
    lean,   [thinner,
  " And now every day makes you grow thinner and

The Humorist.

" I can manage it all, you must have opposition,
    " Must be spurned from the house and have stories
        about you,
" Must be twitted of birth and your lowly condition,
    " And I 'll tell Imogene if she meets you to flout you,
" Then the girl will wake up and will come to her
        senses,
    " Like a sister to brother she 'll fly to defend you,
" She will boast of your birth, and deny your offenses,
    " Then, then you must fall sick, and she 'll want to
        attend you,
" And I 'll make a great fuss, shut her up in the house,
    " Then, then you must propose an elopement and
        marriage,   [mouse,
" She will bite at that bait, she 'll be trapped like a
    " And to make the scene rich, take my horses and
        carriage."

'T was a splendid programme, the performance begun,
    Everything went along as the widow had planned it,
In a couple of weeks she enjoyed the fun,   [it.
    As she looked to the future and narrowly scanned
The elopement and marriage at last were complete,
    If the storms were to come Imogene now could
        brave them,

Boarding Around.

They returned in a week and knelt down at the feet
Of their mother, who freely and frankly forgave
them.

Postscript.

Well, the widow still lives in the hopes she shall
marry—
Mr. Smith is yet teaching the old District School,
Imogene has a fine chubby baby to carry—
I've exhausted the yarn that was wound on my
spool.

Chronicle.

"What curious notions village girls do get,"
Says Sam; "in Newcomb, any good school-master
Could take the cream (excepting one); I'll bet
They'd flock around him sure, thicker and faster
Than bees do around a basswood getting honey,
And wouldn't say a word about his money."

"How different 't is with our St. Regis girls.
When any nice young brave that's decent looking,
Makes love to them, they laugh, and shake their curls;
'The slyest fish is caught with skillful hooking;'
I know a chap," says Nick, "one moonlight night,
Who wooed, and won, and wed a maid at sight."
VI.   1,000

The Humorist.

My friends are tired, *(*in fact have all *re*-tired*)*,
   But in the body only; jokes elastic
Rebound from bunk to bunk, *bon mots* are fired
   Like paper balls in school; the flings sarcastic
Dart here and there like devils darning needles,
Till weary nature sinks and Morpheus wheedles.

Though not a word is spoken in the party,
   Some muttered recollection of the tale
Escapes the lips, half conscious; laughter hearty
   In sudden bursts dies in a sleepy wail;
I think I feel the little drowsy god,
And guess I'd better stop before I nod.

CHAPTER VII.

THE FARMER.

Chronicle.

I think I should have told you in my last,
    I lamed myself and could not take the tramp
My friends proposed; they went, and so I passed
    The days alone, and safely kept the camp;
I lived upon the fishes that I hooked,
And some provision Cæsar left me, cooked.

Since they returned, that is, the last few days,
    The weather has been cool, and damp, and dreary;
I've labored hard upon my boyish lays,
    To make them readable, till often weary
In thinking long of scenes at home; it seems
Almost as real as it does in dreams.

'T is twilight hour; of course, I am on hand,
    And merely lack some one to introduce me;
The grave Professor comes at my command,
    But, in reply, " Dear sir," he says, " excuse me;
You know I cannot do it with propriety,
For you're another *stratum* in society."

The Farmer.

I ask the Traveler, who's seen foreign parts,
   If he can't do the little job for me;
But he replies, "I deal in no fine arts,—
   Politeness is a fine art, do n't you see?"
I ask the Poet; his reply is faster
Than snappish girl's, "Too young, go ask the Master."

And next, I try the learned Engineer,
   And his response, in fact, is quite offensive.
Historian, next, I supplicate in fear;
   He puts himself at once on the defensive:
"Dear sir, we all refuse, can't you see through it?
Because the Master has agreed to do it."

I may not know a word of ancient history;
   I may not comprehend this engineering;
I may not deal in mythologic mystery;
   I never may have traveled out of hearing;
I may not name a pebble in geology;
But I can make a real tip-top apology.

"Our speaker for the night is Secretary
   Of New York Shepherd's State Association;
His duties light, his office honorary;
   He fills with pride the humble situation.
(Thou wilt not hear him, Sam, now, if thou sleepest),
As Artemus Ward would say, "Behold the Sheep-ist!"

Farmer's Apology.

It is not often that a man like Burns,
A farmer born, a farmer bred to toil,
Attempts to court the favors of the Muse,
And weave his rude and rustic thoughts in verse.
It is not often he who plows the fields,
Can plow the field of authorship beside,
And as he culls the flowers on the mead,
Retain the fragrant essence and the hue
Within his brain from which to raise boquets
In aftertimes, and give them to the world.
It is not often one is called to leave
The dirty handle of the plow or spade,
And stand unkempt in simple shepherd's gear,
Before the aged, eloquent and wise.
   Ah! few, indeed, are they whose names can stand
With glory crowned, upon the scroll of fame,
Who sought for inspiration in the fields,
The wood, the hill-top, or the running brook;
Though history tells of now and then a man,
Who rose to eminence from humble life.
Unlike the few we read of, whose grand verse
Extolled the deeds of some heroic chief,
Or trilled their ditties, penned in flaming praise,
Of rustic beauties, or their tender love,
Or, equally as grand, their love of home;
I trembling stand, unequal to my task,
With nought to recommend me to your hearts,
Except some singularity of thought,

The Farmer.

Some odd conceit, or droll, peculiar style,—
A quaint expression or obscure remark.
  My mind for years has quite at random run,
Much like a garden injured by neglect,   [bloom,
Where weeds and flowers commingled, spring and
And sun-flowers flaunt, (a type of ignorance),
Their brazen faces unto all the world ;
Where flow'ring shrubs no pruning knife have known,
And gnarled and knotted grow and blossom rare ;
Where walks and borders overgrown with grass,
Allow no dainty, slippered foot to tread,
With trailing robes, the sinuous way to find,
In shady alcove, or in grotto dark,
The hidden genius of some mystic fount,
Whose falling waters lull no more the soul ;
Where broken vases hold no tropic plants,
And statues, headless, armless, tumbled down
From their pedestals, stained, in ruin lie,
And all that should be elegant and rich
With Nature's beauties, or her hand-maid, Art,
A desert stands,—a blot, a useless waste,
Attractive only like the laurel flowers
That woo the insects with enticing sweets,
And, with their fragrance stupefy their souls.
  I 'm quite unlearned, excepting what I 'm taught
By hard experience of the cares of life ;
The walks of Science I have never trod,
And Art has never known me in her train ;

Farmer's Apology.

Scholastic lore is hidden from my eyes
By sable veil, that covers foreign tongues,
And classic ground is far beyond my reach,
Which Time has thrown a triple wall around,
The Latin, Hebrew, Greek, of ancient days.
　My hour's discourse may represent my farm;
Some fields are fallow, some with forest crowned,
A few in pasture, others sown with grain,
With blooming meadows and the waving corn.
It is not fitted to compete for gold,
Or other prize, at agricultural fair;
The fences are not in the best of shape,
Nor have I taken time to put some things
Oft deemed unsightly in a by-way place;
The burdocks grow beside the garden fence;
The ox-eyed daisy and the prairie flower
Oft show amid the clover's purple bloom,
And thistles often overtop the grain.
You'll notice here and there an ugly stump
Or mighty boulder, cumbering the soil,
A place that needs a drain, a barren knoll
Where plaster should be sown with lavish hand,
And portions, also, where the sub-soil plow
Should break the clayey ridges with its wedge,
And lift them to the action of the frost;
And many things most sadly out of place,
That those of greater skill with plow or pen
Might manage well, and please you better far.
　VII.

A winter's day on Onondaga's hills
   Has charms peculiar to poetic spirits;
The broad and checkered landscape fairly fills
   The soul with pleasure, and if one inherits
A love for Nature in her grandest moods,
   He there can see her in her dress the whitest,
Where graceful swells are robed in darkest woods,
   And icy lakes that sparkle oft the brightest.

The vision bounded by the rising ground,
   Is brown with woods that touch the deep cerulean;
The giant trunks, erect or prostrate, round,
   Withstand or yield to forces most herculean;
The intervening vales of farming land
   Divided are by walls and wooden fences;
In groups the modest farming buildings stand
   Around the home that shows no false pretenses.

The gray-haired shepherd at the noontide hour
   Is filling in the racks his load of fodder;
The sated flock to their accustomed dower
   Approaching slowly, trailing like the dodder,
Their dusky fleeces black by contrast seem,   [know,
   They ne'er were "white as snow," as you and I
But always called so in poetic dream
   Before the advent of Improved Merino.

January—Varieties

Upon convenient tree the carrion crow
  Is watching anxious for a mutton dinner,
That lies half-frozen on a stump below,
  The skinless victim of some mongrel sinner
That prowls nocturnal 'mong the shepherd's flocks,
  Committing oft the worst of bloody slaughter,
A combination of the wolf and fox,
  That ought to die by overdose of water.

See yonder woodman ! hear his ringing stroke ;
  The chips before his bright ax freely flying,
Now cracking, crashing falls the sturdy oak,
  And quick in snowy bed is prostrate lying.
That brave old oak for centuries had stood ;
  How cool its shade has been 'neath branches spreading,
But soon how warm will be the blazing wood,
  Its genial glow and cheering influence shedding.

See yonder toiling team with monstrous load
  Of wood wade through the lane where snow is drifted,
Now up, now down ; the pitches in the road
  Throw off some sticks, but on again they're lifted.
The whistling teamster, as he walks behind,
  Is anxious looking for the sun's declining,
His broken tune denotes perturbed mind,
  His chores will make him late we are divining.

VII.

The Farmer—Skating.

A hemlock stub burns brightly on the shore,
   This beacon calls the boys and girls together
From neighboring hills, and now at least a score,
   With polished steel and flexile straps of leather,
Have reached the lake a happy, merry band,
   To pass the evening pleasantly in skating;
The glary ice is firm from land to land,
   The breeze is bland, their happy hearts elating.

Now writing figures, flourishes and names,
   Or backwards, forwards, circling quite incessant,
The couples swing; his visage fairly flames,
   And she reveals his company is pleasant.
A race! a race! away with merry cheer,
   Like restive steeds, across the lake they 're dashing,
Diverge, converge, or dropping in the rear,
   Each flying footstep like a meteor flashing.

With graceful movements swaying left and right,
   With ease, precision, in their postures placing,
The winning couple come; they lead to-night
   The contra dance, the prize they won a racing.
They dance and play, still whirling like the leaves
   Before the wind, ere polkas were invented,
Till Luna full her southing point achieves,
   Then all trudge home fatigued, but yet contented.

February—Breaking Roads.

The mist, arising from a neighboring lake,
  Is borne across the plain by chilly breezes,
And, rising on the hills, compelled to take
  A higher altitude, it slowly freezes;
The little crystals, rough like salt and fine,
  Will cling to trees and fences, shrubs and buildings,
Till all are white and pure as virgin's shrine;
  But Sol dissolves the diamonds in his gildings.

The common road is drifted full of snow,
  The farmers are assembled now to break it,
(Or get it ready for another blow)
  And fix it well as possible to make it,
With oxen, horses, shovels, harrows, plows;—
  The cattle toil and tug till, fairly smoking,
They've waded through, the horses rearing souse
  With sleighs and plows, with men and boys all joking.

The older ones the polished shovels ply,
  And toss the cakes of snow like walls beside them;
A straight canal they dig where drifts are high;—
  Next come the horses, with the boys to ride them,
Attached to harrows to compress the path,
  Each lad, no doubt, desirous thus to earn a
Sweet compliment from one who showed his wrath
  Because he could not prosecute his journey.
VII.

The Farmer—Coasting.

The road is opened, and the jingling bells
    Proclaim the snow-bound traveler departing,
Who, reared in distant vales or quiet dells,
    At last, with steeds refreshed is homeward starting.
The loaded teams toward the city wend,   [ber
    With hay, and grain, and meat, and wood, and lum-
Oft meeting those who 've little cash to spend,
    With salt and plaster in a goodly number.

The snow is frozen and the crust is thick,   [denses;
    This frequent freezing much the snow con-
The icy hill-side gleams, 't is firm and thick
    Above the tops of e'en the highest fences.
A keen nor'west wind chills the evening air,
    And clears the sky of fleecy clouds' that, flying
Afar to east, obscure the full moon fair;
    The sun descends, their folds with crimson dyeing.

The air is pure, the stars are shining bright;
    The wind already gently is subsiding;
'T is bidding fair to be a lovely night
    For boys and girls upon the hill-side sliding.
Yes, there they gather thickly on the brow,
    And every one the little sled preparing.
"Hold! steady! wait! together, ready, now!"
    Away they fly, the little dangers daring.

February—Coasting.

With laugh and shout the noisy urchins go,
   Till swifter, swifter, they seem almost flying,
Until they reach the distant plain below,
   And then their speed is slower, gently dying.
Now, quickly turning, hasten up the hill
   With steps soon short and shorter, faint and fainter,
They struggle on and up with cheerful will,
   Each pulling, tugging stoutly at his painter.

And now they form a mimic railroad train,
   With all the bustle and the mock confusion;
The larger girls and boys cannot refrain,
   But join the urchins in their dear illusion.
The fastest sled, of course, must go before,
   Then next, and next, till all are others drawing;
One boy must whistle, and a dozen more
   Must make an engine with a wild hurraing.

The slower sleds are baggage cars, and freight,
   To keep the train continuous and steady;
The passengers are in and anxious wait;
   Conductor shouts, "Now, all aboard! All ready!
Go on!" They fly like lightning down the steep,
   Shout, whistle, scream, still going faster, faster,
They wheel, capsize, and make a motley heap,
   But none the worse for their misplaced disaster.

The Farmer—March.

How changed the checkered landscape now appears;
   The southern wind dissolves the cumb'ring snow;
The banks are weeping, and their copious tears
   Increase the brooklets, and the river's flow.
The woods are brown, the fields are nearly bare,
   And look like pictures in great frames of white;
The ling'ring snow-drifts,— saving here and there
   A field of wheat, they seem in barren plight.

The broken fences and the scattered rails,
   Attest their weakness and the strength of wind,
For roving sheep and cattle naught avails,—
   They scale all barriers where the banks are kind.
The withered herbage, damaged by the snow,
   They seek persistent, or some leaf that's green,
And roam unchecked, destroying as they go,
   Unless confined, and each day grow more lean.

How sultry seems the blazing noonday sun,
   How languidly the chopper swings his ax;
The boys no longer yoke the calves for fun,
   The colt for mischief all incitement lacks;
The docile oxen in the cattle yard,
   Contented lie, or ruminating stand,
They stretch beneath the farmer's wiry card,
   Or lick the salt from out his open hand.

Sugar Making.

The early robin whistles from the top-
  Most limb of some domesticated pine ;
The cawing crows their croakings only stop,
Whenc'er they see the farmer with his kine,
Within the thicket dark the partridge drums,
  Or, whirring, starts at some uncommon noise ;
Around the door the honeyed insects hum,
  The pest of girls, the great delight of boys.

The largest maples in the neighboring wood,
  For many years have annually been bled ;
The greed of man, the storms of heaven withstood,
  Again for him their watery sweets they shed.
The trees are tapped, the buckets nearly full,
  The weary plow-boy brings from trees to camp,
With sled and cask, the sap, with tug and pull,
  Or yoke and pails, in toilsome, tedious tramp.

He cuts the wood with many an aching stroke,—
  The toil's fatiguing for such little gains,—
His fire burns badly with most stifling smoke,
  Which illy pays the toiler for his pains.
The thickened syrup, strained and purified,
  Till clear as honey in its amber comb,
Is settled, cleansed, and duly clarified,
  Then cooled and, covered safely, carried home.

The Farmer—Sugar Party.

For all his toil the plow-boy pleasure wins;
    The neighboring young folks are invited there,
And now the sweetest of the sport begins,
    With hearty lads and buxom lasses fair.
They play for kisses in a game of chance,
    Incipient husbands, embryonic wives,
Seem choosing partners in life's contra-dance,—
    Delicious time, the sweetest in their lives.

The "sugaring off" at length is finely done,
    And quick in saucers it is passed around;
They partly stop their frolicking and fun,
    To solve the graining mystery profound.
'Mid laughing, joking, teasing, making wax,
    In pulling candy, or in daubing faces,
All methods of invention sure they tax,
    To make this happiest of all happy places.

Look, if you can, with an unbiased mind,
    On groups of youth and beauty on the floor;
The sugary thoughts are banished from the mind,
    When music floats in sweetest cadence o'er;
Till weary dancing, and the hour grown late,
    Away for homes they happily depart,
Each lad provided with congenial mate,
    Who bless the generous entertainer's heart.

April—Varieties.

The landscape brightens; woods, no longer dun,
    Assume a greener tinge; the meadows, wheat,
And pastures gleaming in the morning sun,
    Have every shade of emerald hue complete.
The unplowed fields with last year's stubble strown,
    Or specked with heaps of compost lately drawn,
Look smutched and dirty; leaves in eddies blown,
    Are being raked, by matrons, from the lawn.

We see the polished plows on upland field,
    Roll up the soil to warming sun and air,
The clods, tenacious, most reluctant yield
    To mellowing harrow trailing shortly there.
The thriving farmer now no longer sows
    His seed-grain broadcast in the open air;
The drill, advancing, plants continuous rows
    Of golden grain, and covers them with care.

The fences now are being well repaired,
    The leaning post made plumb, the broken boards,
Are spliced, the scattered rails replaced,—compared
    With mending broken wall, this fun affords.
Out on the flats they'r putting in the drains,
    The muddy ridges telling where they lie;
The tile are laid with most particular pains,
    To make the field more fruitful when more dry.

VII.

The Farmer—Birds, Fish.

The birds are building nests, *(*they still are few*)*,
   Upon the gable's cornice,—mud and hay,
With wool well lined, the robin builds anew.
   In yonder bar-post, hollowed by decay,
The blue-bird hides her feathers, hair and tow;
   The martin-swallows underneath the eaves,
Construct their muddy huts like Esquimaux;
   Beside a log the partridge builds with leaves.

The red-winged black-bird on the marshy ground,
   Is gleaning cat-tail fuzz to line her nest;
The cautious cat-bird, peering, dodging 'round,
   Though often heard, is rarely seen, at best.
The icy chains are broken in the streams,
   The turbid waters have all passed away,
The brooks are sparkling 'mid the alders; gleams
   Of broken sunlight with the ripples play.

Now, up the streams the finny squadrons take
   Their annual journey to the highest source,
And leave the deeper waters of the lake
   In countless numbers and unreckoned force.
The larger children leave the school and books,—
   Perchance it may with them be holiday,—
And gather lines, and poles, and tiny hooks,
   And for the nearest trout-stream hie away.

April—Fishing.

With sanguine hearts fast beating in each breast,
    They join their playmates, eager for the sport,
Some thinking this, and some that stream the best,
    But all agreeing in the " fish report."
They 've found the spot from marching long about,
    The hooks are baited, a most treacherous trap,
The eager eyes are sparkling, looking out
    For speckled beauties' quick, voracious snap.

The girls get bothered; and get pricked with hooks,
    Their lines get tangled and quite often fast,
They can't impale a worm, but by their looks
    They show that they're impaled themselves at last.
Though making havoc with the scaly tribe,
    They 're making greater conquest with the boys.
With merry laugh and teasing, tickling gibe,
    They scare the fish, which no true beau annoys.

The baskets filled with fattest fish, all dressed,
    They start for home, as " hungry as the dogs;"
A sudden shower comes sweeping from the west,
    And soaks them all as thoroughly as bogs.
They reach their homes and have their meal of fish,
    Enjoyed far more perhaps by being rare,
For appetite gives zest to every dish,—
    The daintiest item in each bill of fare.

The Farmer—May.

The woodland slopes are clothed in deepest green,
　The vocal tenants tireless tune their lays;
In deep seclusion, heard, but seldom seen,
　They build their nests, well hid by leafy sprays.
The hawk, or crow, on some majestic pine,
　Secures its nest from man's keen searching eye.
Some hollow trunk holds, darker than a mine,
　The screech-owl's brood, profoundly wise and sly.

Up in some tow€ring maple's blasted trunk,
　The high-hoie digs the pocket for her nest;
The little carpenter shows lots of spunk,
　And drives her chisel, rarely taking rest.
The fields are vocal with the feathered choir,
　The bob-o-link, the clown of birds, has come,
The golden oriole flits, a flash of fire,　　　[home.
　Through drooping elms where hangs his hammock

Some fields are taking on a deeper hue,
　And those so brown, the brighter shades of green;
Some barren still remain; lines straight and true
　Reveal the cross where corn hills will be seen.
The guardian angel dressed in wretched plight,
　The dangling cobs, the scraps of glittering tin,
Secure the corn from thieving crows; the fright
　Has slight addition in the windmill's din.

May—Varieties.

Up on the hills, in dirty white, the flocks
    Have flecked the pastures, grazing quiet, still,
The lambs run races, gambol o'er the rocks,
    Till bleating mothers call them at their will.
The cattle on the flats, with filthy flanks
    And shaggy coats half shed, in quiet graze;
The logy plow-team play their teasing pranks,
    And seemingly enjoy their holidays,

The garden, now the sire's peculiar care,
    Begins to show each little fringe of green ;
The lettuce, beets and onions springing there,
    Have pestering weeds continually between.
The early peas are bushed in ragged lines,
    Asparagus grows rankly from the stool,
Glass-covered boxes shield the tender vines
    From striped bugs and weather over cool.

The lawn is trimmed, the flower-beds are raked,
    The tiny seeds are planted, and the pots
Of house-plants scattered; slender ones are staked
    With care, located in protected spots.
The lily, peony and daffodil,
    With tulip, dahlia, pansy, flower-de-luce,
And flowering shrub, some plot or border fill,
    Too often thought to be of doubtful use.

The Farmer—May-Day.

The wild flowers blossom in the woods and fields
   In fine profusion, where no cattle roam ;
The young folks gather on the "green," their peals
   Of ringing laughter tell us whence they come ;
With willow baskets, scissors, twine and tape,
   The boys with knives, the girls with needles keen,
They're armed to wander, gather flowers to drape
   The bower of beauty—crown the young May Queen.

In couples now they gaily sally out,
   To gather trophies from the wooded dell ;
The girls go laughing, boys with boist'rous shout,
   But soon subdued, these, blushing, trembling, tell
The honied story, old, but ever new.
   They make their double garlands and boquets,
With trailing cedar, hemlock, ivy, yew,
   And pass the happiest hour in all their days.

Once more assembled on the school house green,
   With treasures they have gathered for the bower,
The myrtle wreath to crown the blushing queen,
   By all acknowledged as their fairest flower.
The leafy grottoes built, the throne bedight
   With emerald chains and flowers in garlands gay ;
With hands all joined 'round her, in voice unite,
   Proclaiming SABRA as the Queen of May.

June—Washing Sheep.

The landscape now is clothed in royal robes,
 The rising hills with densest foliage crowned,
The fields with grass and grain, the crimson globes
 In orchard rows shed fragrance rich around.
The wheat is shooting up its earliest heads,
 Its purple bloom the early clover shows,
Inviting myriad bees, and essence sheds,—
 In light green ranks the cornfields show their rows.

The shepherd calls his flock with tempting salt,
 And toles them to the pen beside the brooks,
Whose course is turned, preventing thus the fault
 Which gives to greasy fleeces dingy look.
The vat o'erflows, the flock is made secure,
 A half a dozen are thrown in together
To soak, till washed by men and made quite pure,
 Then dripping ewes return with old bell-wether.

See two boys tugging with the broad-horned ram;
 They push and pull, he simply stubs and braces,—
He's been their pet, perhaps, from little lamb,
 But faster grown than they; their crimson faces
With perspiration flushed, and crystal beads,
 They persevere and in the water souse him;
With bleating cries he piteously pleads,
 Till they release him, take him home and house him.

The Farmer—Shearing.

A fortnight later, and the great barn floor
   Presents to us an animated scene,
And easy viewed through broad and open door.
   The space is swept most scrupulously clean.
Beside the benches bow the men with shears,
   Above the sheep that carefully each clips;
The ewes uneasy, show their natural fears
   Of clicking noise, or more vexatious nips.

A fleece is dropped, a wether fairly bounds
   Toward the pasture, looking white as snow,
With beauty vanished, lank and lean as hounds,—
   The frightened lambs their mothers scarcely know.
Next, on the table are the fleeces laid,
   Extraneous things removed; with careful fold
Are put in press and tied, released and weighed;
   The snowy cubes are ready for the gold.

The little lake well sheltered by the wood,
   That long reflected back the noonday sun,
Absorbed in time the calorific flood,
   Until at length it fairly has begun
To feel a genial glowing in its breast,—
   A pleasing warmth through all its coves and caves;
The sweltering boys of all their clothes divest,
   From rocky ledge now plunge beneath its waves.

June—Swimming.

The timid ones still stand upon the bank,
  And watch the skillful as they're striking out,
Now venture in upon some trusted plank,
  But tremble still between desire and doubt.
Emboldened much, with confidence restored,
  Between two older ones to succor him,
The tyro drops at length his little board,
  And, proudly conscious, he has learned to swim.

The springing plank is placed beneath a rock,
  And o'er a log high points the other end;
Now, creeping up like frogs, you see them flock,
  And with their weight the stubborn timber bend.
Now, springing, springing, hear the groaning ash;
  Up! up, they fly above the crystal tide,
And turn in air, headforemost, with a splash,
  Divide the waves, then, rising, puff with pride.

The old farm mansion's handsome, close-mown lawn
  Is gay with noisy girls who play croquet;
The more sedate to Flora's bower are drawn,
  Each busy fashioning a sweet boquet.
The boys return from bathing just in time
  To see them safely home in twilight's hour,
The roseate time of love in our cool clime,
  When sweetness dwells in every grove and bower.

The Farmer—*July*.

The morn is ushered by the booming gun,
    That sends its welcome from the distant town,
To rouse the patriot spirits ere the sun
    Has changed the eastern sky to red from brown.
The birds, awakened by unusual noise,
    Much more melodious chant their little lays,
The cannon, pistols, crackers of the boys,
    Announce the chief of Yankee holidays.

Now all is bustle; chores dispatched with speed—
    The team is caught and curried, fed with meal,
The cows, half-milked, are turned away to feed,
    The pigs, forgotten, left till night to squeal.
In little time potatoes peeled and boiled,
    With ham and eggs, *(*the minstrel's latest *lay,)*
But breakfast barely tasted, dishes soiled,
    Are slipped into the cupboard for the day.

The team is harnessed to the carry-all,
    The girls in gayest dresses and bright shoes,
Like rose-buds sweet, the boys, both great and small,
    With neighbors' sons can foot it as they choose.
The gray-haired farmer drives the restive bays,
    The robust matron sitting by his side,
With anxious eye her family surveys,
    And smiles approving with a conscious pride.

July—Celebration.

The village green is mottled with the throng,
  The bell is ringing in the church's steeple,
The marshal and his aids ride right and wrong
  In trying to arrange untutored people;
The village band advance, (a fife and drum),
  Militia, next Good Templars' sweet communion,
With thirty-six white dressed young ladies come,
  With handsome flags, insignia of our Union.

Next, carriages with some distinguished leader
  Of "eighteen twelve" with comrades by his side,
The clergy, poet, orator and reader,
  And next our heroes, who should ever ride,
Who won their honors on a southern soil;
  And followed nobly by a lengthy train,
All seek the grove where youth, with faithful toil,
  A stand have built and seats spread on the plain.

The crowd is hushed; we hear the fervent prayer,
  The Declaration firmly, fairly read,
The long oration, (oft in pompous air),
  The poet's lay, and benediction said,
The company disperse; where tables creak
  With such substantials as the country yields,
They all are welcome to partake who seek
  The viands of the forests or the fields.
VII.

The Farmer—The Ride and Ball.

Some twenty buggies, and in each a twain,
  All gaily dressed, well trimmed with evergreen,
The dashing horses, bearing on the rein,
  Departing from the village can be seen.
They ride, perhaps, to view some cascade fair,
  Some lake's lone beach, to search for tiny shells
To deck their dresses or adorn their hair,
  In imitation of the Indian belles.

The village inn is fairly in a blaze,
  From every window gleams the mellow light,
The crowd of loafers idly gaping, gaze
  As rustic beauties blushingly alight.
The viol's music in bewitching tones,
  In broken strains floats on the evening air,
The soul reviving in some old man's bones,
  Who sees the girls go tripping up the stair.

They dance unceasing till the little hours,
  By waning moon admonished to refrain;
Till weary Nature's over-burdened powers
  Refuse to keep in concord with the strain,
The steeds are brought, they leave by diverse ways,
  The sleepy beau his horse scarce keeping straight,
Must claim his tribute, which she freely pays,
  They kiss and part beside her father's gate.

August—Haying.

No nobler sight can mortal ever view
In rural scene, than Onondaga hills
Can oft afford; no sky can be more blue,
Nor slopes more graceful, and no brighter rills;
But grandest time of all the varying year,
  Is just before the haying is complete,
When men and beasts most busily appear,
  All hurried by the early ripening wheat.

The fallow's black, manured with mucky ground,
  Deep darkly green the woods, the oats and corn,
The flax pale blue, neglected clover browned
  By ripening heads, where golden seeds are born.
The ripening grain has every yellow shade,
  From Guinea gold down to a faded green,
The lemon, orange, amber, Indian Maid,
  Or Octoroon, and dozens more between.

See yonder meadow just three-quarters mown,
  One-fourth is drawn and added to the stock,
Another fourth lies flat, by Tedder thrown,
  The other fourth is windrowed, or in cock.
Around the fence an old-time mower swings,—
  The spanking bays come dancing through the gate,
The bar is dropped, the Clipper Mower rings.
  And knows no wages—frets not when 't is late.

The Farmer—Haying.

Now following soon the kicking Tedder comes,
  And in the air the emerald bunches flings;
The Sulky Horse-rake cleans the ground like combs,
  And gathers windrows with its steely springs.
Some men are opening out the cocks to dry,
  From last night's windrows shaking off the dew,
A bumble-bee makes one young urchin fly,—
  He gets the bitter with the sweet, 't is true.

A part is dry and can be taken in,
  The wagon 's coming with the men and forks,
The loose boards rattling make a vexing din,
  And noisy boys,—now every school-boy works.
The heavy forkfulls rise upon the rack,
  The loader treading builds it true and square,
The sides keeps equal, guided by the track,
  The boys behind with hand-rakes glean with care.

They reach the barn, roll in upon the floor,
  The men and boys ascend the sweltering mow,
An active horse stands by the open door,
  He starts the fork, and pulleys rattle now.
From horse to load the rope by rafter leads,
  The great heap rises o'er the purline beam,
A click! 't is dropped; another soon succeeds;
  'T is off! and almost easy as a dream.

August—Harvesting.

We view again this scene a few days hence,
   In harvest days, with men, and boys, and teams,
The stalwart cradler cutting by the fence,
   The horses' pathway very narrow seems.
The flaming Champion Reaper follows soon,
   Around the field a Harvest Hymn it sings,
The ripe grain falls as in a sudden swoon,
   The strong rake travels its eccentric rings.

The golden gavels in continuous rows
   Lie loose, but square, to tempt the binder's art,
With rakes of ash they open bunches close,
   And often double when not far apart.
The straightened handful, with peculiar twist,
   Is formed a band and wrapped the sheaf around,
Is siezed by left hand under, crossed by wrist,
   Is twisted, kinked, tucked under and is bound.

By boys the sheaves in shocks are careful placed,
   In dozens, twenties, or sometimes fifteens,
With due precision, so that none may waste,
   In double tiers, with little space between.
The scorching sun soon makes the berry hard,
   The sheaves on wagon to the barn are rolled,
Where prudent farmers, who have much regard
   For well lined pockets, turn them into gold.

VII.

The Farmer—September.

The harvesting of grass and grain is done,
    And only corn and clover seed remain;
The fields look frizzled, save the brownest one,—
    That's being sown with drill to winter grain.
The pasture lots are looking bare and brown,
    The rowen has not started, for the drouth;
The corn, late sown for fodder, must come down
    When waiting cattle water at the mouth.

That wheat or barley must be threshed for space
    For corn or clover, clearly can be seen;
Ten fine stout horses walk with steady pace
    The little circle, driving the machine,
Within the barn, where dirty men and boys
    Are hid by dust, and smoke, and straw, and chaff,
The thresher's hum, the separator's noise,
    Will din your ears until you think you're daff.

From highest peak the bundles tumbling come,
    By nimble boy arranged, who cuts the bands;
The feeder holds them where the steel teeth hum,
    And gradually draw them from his hands.
The straw goes on a carrier to the stack,
    The chaff and grain are dropped where cooling blast
With shaking sieves and screens in awful clack,
    Completely clean it, then in bin 't is cast.

September—Harvest Home.

Of all the themes by anxious poets sought,
  Of all the scenes in fairy land portrayed,
Of all the pictures fancy ever wrought,
  Of all the visions dreamers ever made,—
No happier sight ere blest a mortal eye,
  No grander scene transpires neath starry dome;
To write its praise my pen would soon run dry,
  And fail to tell you of our Harvest Home.

Here youth and beauty budding into bloom;
  Here manhood's prime and manhood in decay;
Here age enfeebled, ripening for the tomb,
  The youthful mother and the matron gray;
The nursing babes, the gay school-girls and boys,
  In comprehensive view we easy scan;
'Mid sorrows, cares, anxieties and joys,—
  A panorama of the life of man.

Within a handsome grove whose cooling shade,
  With balmy fragrance filled, the people meet;
Their contributions are on tables laid,
  Which some committee will arrange complete.
In various ways they pass the afternoon;
  The children swing, the boys can play bass ball,
The girls croquet; the old enjoy their boon
  Of pleasant converse, till the supper call.
VII.

The Farmer—Harvest Home.

The table 's spread for many hundred feet,
  The bell is rung, the hungry crowd attend,
Where fruit and flowers with viands rare and sweet,
  Are in abundance piled from end to end.
The feast is o'er, the witty with their toast,
  A speech, or story, anecdote or song,
Amuse till sun-down the departing host,
  Except the youthful, who their mirth prolong.

Upon a stand the bonfire blazes high,
  And casts its glow upon the dancing floor;
A crimson tinge it gives to trees and sky,
  And covers beauty's cheek with blushes o'er.
The music softened or absorbed by trees,
  The swaying dancers in their dresses gay;
The odorous woodland, all combine to please,
  And rouse the soul with their ecstatic sway.

From this fair scene a poet might indite
  A fairy tale, with fancy flowing free;
Each girl a nereid in sea robes bedight,—
  The grove a coral grotto of the sea.
The boys the elves, the sky the bright blue waves,
  The music echoes from Plutonian shore,
The feeble light, Tartarus' lurid caves,
  The evening breeze a tempest's mellowed roar.

October—The Woods.

Jack Frost, the cunning, icy-hearted wight,
   Is creeping through our valleys, o'er our hills.
Like prowling thief, in silence and at night,
   He comes, and tender vegetation kills.
The woods have donned their holiday attire,
   As gorgeous in their hues as Flora's bower,
Or rainbow tint, or night's electric fire,
   Or clouds sun-painted in the twilight hour.

The old soft maple in the marshy ground,
   Is clothed in scarlet, black ash by its side
Has hue of slate; the alders are just browned,
   The ivy flaunts magenta plumes in pride.
The water birch a lemon yellow wears,
   And in deep contrast with the cedar's green,
The drooping elm a salmon vestment bears;
   The blue beech in its fawn-drab cloak is seen.

Upon the hills the sugar-maples take
   Their robes of crimson, ash, a claret brown;
The basswood draped in maize, the dwarfed sumach
   Has solferino-colored morning gown;
The royal purples wrap the several oaks,
   (Black, white, and red), mauve, violet, and blue.
The sassafras seems spotted by the skokes;
   Beech, birch and chestnut dress in orange hue.

The Farmer—Cider.

Within the orchard little girls and boys
  Are picking apples from beneath a tree,
Where larger ones, anticipate the joys
  That they'll partake of at the paring bee.
The fairest, smoothest, roundest of the lot,
  Are picked with care and handled, too, with skill;
The small, with bruised ones, those inclined to rot
  Are placed in wagons for the cider mill.

You know the mill is near before you look,
  You smell the pomace piled beside the fence,
You see the barrels soaking by the brook,   [vents.
  The boys with straws are sucking through the
The load is carried to an upper door
  And lifted oft to inconvenient height,
Where fifty kinds are strewn upon the floor
  To wait the day when precedence gives right.

The lazy horse goes 'round, the creaking wheels,
  With bands and gearing, make the grater hum
That eats all sorts, nor stops for cores or peels,
  But makes a mush of all the kinds that come.
The pomace lying in its bed of juice
  A night, assumes a richer amber hue,
Is then removed, the cider like a sluice,
  In freedom flows when urged by mighty screw.

October—Paring-Bee.

The evening shades are thick, the dodging lights
    Among the trees around the house and lawn,
Announce it one of those delightful nights   [dawn
    When young folks meet; e'en since the morning's
They've been preparing, and at last are here.
    The rude old mansion rings with laughter sweet,
The hum of preparation, hearty cheer
    Of new arrivals, sound of pattering feet.

No words can paint this busiest of scenes:
    The skillful hands are paring off the rind
From fragrant fruit, with patented machines;
    Around them sitting, woven, intertwined,
Are happy boys and girls, with dishes filled;
    Some quarter, more must core, a few must string.
The cider's passed in plenty, some gets spilled
    Where fun abounds, and peals of laughter ring.

When labor's done the floor is cleaned of chips,
    No carpet bothers where the dainty feet
Must nimbly fly in rural plays, and skips
    The agile plow-boy, quick of thought and fleet.
Delightfully the golden moments pass,
    An hour or two perhaps in harmless play,
When all go home, each laddie with his lass,
    The late moon rising lighting up their way.
VII.

The Farmer—November.

This is the glorious Indian Summer season,
    These are our sober, sleepy, smoky days;
We feel the breathing of the slightest breeze on
    The highest hill, its sigh a prayer of praise.
There is a dreamy glimmer in the air,
    That gives a languid feeling to the soul,
That takes no note of time, nor aught of care,—
    Our lazy frames admit of no control.

The little children hastening to the school
    In silence, sullen, scarcely think of play,
With naught to tempt a disregard of rule,
    With drooping heads they plod their tedious way.
No story interests them in their books,
    Their minds are murky as the darkest ink,
The puzzled teacher yawns with stupid looks,
    And wonders why she cannot talk or think.

We hear no bleating of the grazing flocks,
    The lambs no longer gambol, skip or play,
The plowman urges not the patient ox
    That, plodding slowly, turns the stubborn clay.
We hear no lowing of the distant herds,
    Or hum of insects, (*'t is their long repose*),
Or soul-delighting chant, the song of birds,
    The neigh of horses, or the caw of crows.

November—Husking.

The trees have shed their many-colored leaves,
    But ripened nuts still hang in plenty 'round,
The nimble-footed squirrels, sly as thieves,
    From branches clip and drop them to the ground.
The keen-eyed sportsman sees the squirrel spring,
    Or hears the pattering nuts with bated breath;
He silent creeps (a most contemptuous thing),
    And makes one sound that only ends in death.

There seems a little movement in the corn,
    The farmer and his men among the stooks
Have been at work e'en since the early morn,
    In stripping husks, with noise like rustling books.
The bright round pumpkin makes convenient seat,
    The unhusked bundle lies across the knee,
The stalks for fodder tied again complete,
    The well filled wagon and the baskets, see!

The richest acre that the big boys own,
    They planted, hoed, and topped with greatest care,
At length makes payment, or returns the loan,
    For time and patience in its treasure rare.
From yellow stalks the silvery ears are snapped,
    And tossed in baskets, taken to the load,
The husks around the red ears closely wrapped,
    Are sure to pay for carefulness bestowed.

The Farmer—Husking Bee.

The great barn door at early candle light,
   A much enlivened scene again presents,
The farmer's there to see that all is aight,—
   That lights are safe from unseen accidents.
The heap of corn is stretched across the floor,
   Not high or broad, and boys profusely plenty,
With shouts come trooping through the open door,
   With girls whose ages range from ten to twenty.

On husks in bunches they recline like Turks,
   And strip the masks from off their golden faces,
The choice ears sending where the farmer works,
   To braid his next year's seed in handsome traces.
When boys a red ear find, with still delight
   They slily put it, (no one seems offended),
In some girl's pocket, thus he wins the right
   To see her safely home when husking's ended.

When all is done the floor is swept quite clean,
   In plays and dances then they take delight;
No costly silk in dresses can be seen,
   But all in modest calico bedight.
Sweet apples, cider, pumpkin pie and cake,
   Are passed in plenty, eaten from the hand;
With due decorum all the lunch partake,
   Then wend their homeward ways, a happy band.

December—Varieties.

The gloomiest time in all the rolling year
   Has swept unnoticed 'round our rural home;
The woodland slopes look dull and dark and drear,
   And sheep and cattle now no longer roam
O'er fields of frozen herbage, blanched and brown.
   The crows are seldom seen; the chattering jay
Is heard in hemlock glen, with curious crown;
   The early snow-bird, startled, flits away.

The mansion's banked with straw, the barn and sheds
   Have doors replaced and windows made secure;
Sheep, horses, cattle, pigs, have strawy beds,
   With food in plenty, water clear and pure.
The farmer draws from out the frozen swamp,
   Across the fields, o'er rough and hubby roads,
And piles them in the yard, all black and damp,
   The muck and marl in many mighty loads.

The scientific youth with active brains,
   Is making searches for the unseen springs,—
With chain and level lays his plans for drains,
   And sticks his stakes for tile to lay in strings.
The oxen haul, perhaps with great expense,
   Some mighty boulder yet unharmed by fire,
To make foundation for the great stone fence,
   But stopping very often to respire.

The Farmer—Snow Storm.

Some two weeks later come the holidays,
    And anxious youth, young women and young men,
Are pleased, for Earth her snowy robe displays
    Upon the hills, in every glade and glen;
The little drifts blown through the rails and walls
    With curious curves, fantastic plumes and scrolls;
The children breaking paths, or rolling balls,
    Or building men and forts upon the knolls.

The evergreens bend graceful with the snow,
    The pines and cedars growing in the swales;
It clings to withered beech and bends it low,
    Whose limber limbs sway easy with the gales.
It lies on basswood, oak, and maple limbs,
    Or hangs like moss upon the roughened side,
The stumps wear night caps, more superb it trims
    The dark green hemlock,—decks it like a bride.

The belles are fully robed in gayest dresses,
    With flounce and furbelows on basques and sacks,
And gimp, and lace, and ribbons; it expresses
    Barbaric relic, which no nation lacks.
The females will wear gewgaws the world over,
    When very young they're dazzled with the glare;
When older grown to fascinate some lover,
    And next, to drive some rival to despair.

December Wedding Party.

The beaux are dressed, too, in their best store clothes,
   And just a little shade above the dandy,
With gloves too small, and boots that pinch their toes,
   And other things unmentionable, but handy.
These belles and beaux in pairs, each in a cutter
   Behind a span of spanking grays or bays,
Seem suited each for each, like bread and butter,
   To pass the gayest of their holidays.

Before the village inn once more they meet,—
   The self-same parties who, some months ago,
In gay procession started down the street,
   Again start out upon the spotless snow.
Toward the city now they speed their way,
   " The tintinabulation of the bells"
In music drowns the sweetest words they say,
   And spoils report of tales each fellow tells.

The loves first spoken on that day in May,
   Have, in some cases, been well fed and cherished;
A few, neglected, droop in sere decay,
   And fewer still, ah! utterly have perished.
Two faithful hearts have beat in union long,
   Resolved no longer to postpone the day,
With sober faces lead the jovial throng,
   To seek the aid of Reverend Doctor May.
VII.

The Farmer—Chronicle.

My friends have visited old John Brown's grave,
   That lies about twelve miles due north from here,
A Mecca where each soul that, born a slave,
   Should dew the turf with sympathetic tear.
A patriot's shrine where all can tribute pay,
In prayer, in anthem, eulogy, or lay.

They toiled a day in Adirondack Pass,
   Among the mighty masses at its base,
With terror viewed the cliff, which, of its class,
   Is one of Nature's wonders; its bare face
Of perpendicular rock a thousand feet
Looms to the sky, majestic, grand, complete.

They visited the famous Preston Ponds,
   A string of pearls upon a silver tress;
The bright Cold River. Nothing corresponds,
   So Sam affirms, in all this wilderness;
With its borean waves it chills the blood
On warmest days when bathing in its flood.

They climbed old Sandanona; from its top
   Could view a dozen little lakes and more,—
See mountains rise around, see river drop
   O'er little cascades, hear the Racket's roar;
And in the east some fields made clean by tillage,
Round Adirondack,—lone deserted village.

CHAPTER VIII.

THE CHOWDER PARTY.

Chronicle.

Our month has fled, and still we linger here,
   Awaiting teams to take us to the lake,
But still contrive to keep up our good cheer,
   For every one desirous seems to make
His neighbor happy, and himself as well;
The way we do it shortly I will tell.

To-day we've all been telling funny stories,
   Excepting Sam, who's gone to get some powder;
'T is plain enough that each narrator glories
   In adding to this intellectual chowder.
Some comic anecdote, or story odd,
In salmagundi—hotch-pot—ollapod.

We have resolved that on to-morrow night,
   If it is fair, (the last we stay in camp),
To make the woodland ring with our delight,
   With old-time songs that bear the genuine stamp
Of our true feelings, gushings of the soul,
When joy or sorrow held complete control.

Chowder.

The wished-for time is here; 't is twilight hour,
    The air is cool, the sky is blue and clear,
And looks just washed by summer's thunder shower,
    There is a freshness in the atmosphere,—
An indescribable metallic ring,
That seems to aid the voice whene'er we sing.

The Chowder Party, which includes the ten,
    Is ready to contribute due proportion
Of fish, flesh, fowl or fruit to fellow-men,
    As ready, also, each will take his portion.
They lay their free-will offerings on the dresser—
And first we listen to the old Professor.

The Gold Hunter—A Cantata.

Part One—Parting.

The first blush of morning that burst from its fountains,
    And over the landscape triumphantly rolled,
Fell soft as the zephyrs on Salisbury's mountains,
    Enrobing their summits in crimson and gold.
The wood on the hill-side looked mournful and hazy,
    The meadows were clothed in the richest of green,
The sloops on the Hudson moved lonely and lazy,
    And only the warblers enlivened the scene.

The Gold Hunter.

At home on the hill-side a couple were standing
And bidding farewells, for it might be for years,
The steamboat bell rung as she neared to the landing,
Which filled the bright eyes of the maiden with tears.
They parted at last as he fondly caressed her,
And promised his absence could, should not be long,
Tho' tears dimmed his eyes as he fervently blessed her,
Light-hearted and gay was the style of his song.

Part Two—The Song.

Far, far away, love, far, far away, love,
From you I go, with friend or foe, come weal or woe, blow high or low,
Far, far away, love, my journey now doth lay, love,
Over the Rocky Mountains far the Eldorado lies.
Alas, the road is long, my heart you know is strong,
The buck or doe, and buffalo will help us well along,
And ere a year has rolled I'll roll in wealth untold,
Tho' all the world oppose me, for gold! gold!! gold!!!

When I return, love, when I return, love,
The friends I meet, will kindly greet, my wand'ring feet, with welcome sweet; [love,
When I return, love, then, oh, then you'll learn,
Wherein this mighty magic of the Eldorado lies.
Friends will want to borrow, I'll bid them "call to-morrow," [their sorrow,
From day to day I'll turn away, and teach them to
I am not of their mold, my friendship is not sold,
And yet I'll rise to eminence on gold! gold!! gold!!!

Chowder.

Part Three—*Trouble.*

He was lost and had wandered a week on the plain,
    And in vain, to discover the trail;
He was journeying slow, for his feet gave him pain,
    And his strength was beginning to fail;
For no food had he known, and he laid himself down,
    With his rifle safe under his head,
In the lee he had found by some sufferer's mound,
    And in fear that he soon would be dead.

But a wolf crossed his track like a hound on the trail,
    How she bounded like light o'er the green,
Half famished, she scented a feast on the gale,
    And his capture might easy have been;
But he hears her soft tread; as he raises his head,
    The baffled wolf quailed, turned to run;
But the rifle's cold lead laid her low with the dead,—
    He was saved and the victory won.

Part Four—*Success.*

I left old Columbia a long way behind me,
    The girl that I loved, and the friends I held dear;
The passion for gold so completely did blind me,
    I forfeited wealth for its counterfeit here.
I've dared every danger and learned to my sorrow,
    That riches bring care to the wisest of men;
As yonder gay steamer will leave here to-morrow,
    I'm bound to go back to Columbia again.

The Gold Hunter.

The wealth I have won must yet purchase me pleasure,
    I'll live like a prince in a palace of stone,
My summer of life with my heart's dearest treasure,
    Must now pass in sunshine, the clouds have all flown. [borrow,—
Old friends will flock 'round me and new ones, to
    I'll help only those who are poorest of men.
As yonder gay steamer will leave here to-morrow,
    I'm bound to go back to Columbia again.

Part Five—Return.

A noble steamer plowed its way,
    Along the placid Hudson's wave;
Upon her deck the Hunter lay,
    By fever worn till nought could save.
A friend was watching by his side,
    And often strove to banish gloom
And give him hope; in vain he tried,
    For he was all too near his tomb.

"Awaken, Tom, your home's in sight,
    And Mary's standing on the shore."
His face beamed with a heavenly light,—
    A light that never shone before.
His cheek is pressed, his form she clasps,
    As languidly he lifts his eyes,—
Returns the kiss, then faintly gasps,
    And in the arms of Mary, dies.

VIII.

Chowder.

"Well, that's a dish of hash that you've presented,
   A little mirth, but more of grief and sadness;
I'll tune you one reversed, not all invented,
   Where misery is turned to joy and gladness."
I glean their scattered straws like faithful gaveler,
So next we'll listen to the tonguy Traveler.

The Old Bachelor.

Once I stopped at a house where a bachelor dwelt;
   Tangled grass had grown up round his door;
I distinctly remember how strangely I felt,
   For I never had felt so before.
He'd a surly old mastiff that saw me approach,—
   In a dismal and sorrowful tone   [encroach,—
Oh, he howled, so it seemed, "do n't you know you
   My old master would live all alone."

Then I glanced o'er the yard so confessedly drear,
   Where there was not a shrub nor a tree,
Not a sign of a plant nor a flower did appear,
   Nor an ornament that I could see.
His old shutters were shattered, the glazing was gone,
   O'er the window sill mosses had grown,
While the sash held a dozen old garments in pawn;
   Ah! thinks I, he must live all alone.

The Old Bachelor.

Then I rapped with the head of my cane on the door,
    And he hastened to usher me in,
Where the dogs by the dozen and cats by the score
    Set up such an unwelcoming din
That I truly was vexed at their hideous noise,
    Till he gave each a quieting bone;
Now if puppies and cats are a bachelor's joys,
    He could not have been living alone.

On his table that stood in the midst of the floor,
    Were a great many dishes unsound,
That were left as unwashed as when dinner was o'er,
    If except what grimalkin had found. [chair,
He had placed me a broken-backed, three-legged
    One that did most beseechingly moan
In a fine variation to "popular air,"
    And especially one all alone.

His old coat had been coated with many a patch,
    Which had likewise invested his vest;
He had mended each breach in his breeches to match,
    And his shirt was a shift with the rest.
But his boot to describe! it is bootless for me;
    He had stock in his stockings unknown;
Oh! his cap capped the climax, and thus, "cap-a-pie,"
    It is true that I found him alone.

Chowder.

Ah! his eyeballs were sunken, their luster was dimmed,
  His pale cheeks were quite hollow and thin;
His dark hair was unshorn, and his whiskers un-
    trimmed,
  Had begun to grow gray on his chin.
He had told me his name, given wealth and his age,
  'T was between a half-sigh and a groan;
When I asked for his wife why he flew in a rage,
  And then left me to guess all alone.

But a few days ago I 'd a task to attend,
  And I had to be passing that way;
Now, thinks I, "I shall see my old bachelor friend,—
  We have not met for many a day."   [bright,
Think how changed was the view, and how beautif'ly
  Now it truly would scarcely be known,
For a statelier mansion was crowning the site;
  Ah! thinks I, "he 's not living alone."

The great yard was well filled with the handsomest
    trees,
  And a graveled walk led to the door,   [breeze,"
Where the flowering shrubs "shed their sweets on the
  Where the flowers did not blossom before.
Now no surly dog met me in guarding the house,
  For he was not a miser 't was known;
He now needed no cats for there was not a mouse,
  And he was not then living alone.

The Old Bachelor.

Oh, how blest was the scene when I rapped at the door,
    And a woman in smiles asked me in,
When the babies were playing with toys on the floor,
    With my friend neither haggard nor thin.
He was dressed quite genteel, he was younger in looks,
    He spake out in a happier tone,
" Please come in, Mr. Census Man, open your books,
    For you 'll find I 'm not living alone."

There his well arranged parlor was ample and neat,
    Filled with furniture brought from afar,
The rich voice of his wife was exquisitely sweet,
    When accompanied with her guitar.
I retired with regret from the beautiful spot,
    Where true happiness only is known ;
Ah ! I envy that quiet old Benedict's lot,
    And have vowed I 'd not live all alone.

" A truthful scene, no doubt, and very pleasant,
    I think I guess the secret of the change.
Old hawks, you know, admire a tender pheasant,
    That girls like wealth in these days is not strange.
When old men fall in love, they like to show it,
The young can 't help it." Let us hear the Poet.

Beautiful Eyes.

Oh ! I know a young woman neither angel nor human,
    But a something between that is almost divine,
I acknowledge with pleasure, aye, and that beyond measure,

Chowder.

That I should be delighted if she could be mine.
For this heavenly creature in her mind, voice and feature, [skies,
Although born of the earth seems a child of the
And her chiefest attraction, one that gives me distraction,
Is the light óf her beautiful, beautiful eyes.

I have met them in gladness, and have left them in sadness, [in hate,
I 've observed them in hope, and have watched them
I have noticed sly glances, as when flurried by fancies,
The long lashes would droop and the pupils dilate.
I have seen them when love made them mild as a dove,
Melting tender with pity that did not despise,
I have looked with devotion on each heartfelt emotion,
As revealed in her beautiful, beautiful eyes.

Oh ! the first time I met her she just fastened a fetter
All about my poor heart that had never been chained,
And so deftly around were the silken cords bound,
It was useless to struggle,—content I remained.
Though appearing affrighted she soon seemed as delighted,
As a child would appear when receiving a prize,
For there was no alloy in that look of pure joy,
As expressed in her beautiful, beautiful eyes,

Beautiful Eyes.

As I once sat down by her, but not thinking to try her,
    I just mentioned 't was tattled "that she was en-
        gaged";   [lashes
The indignant, bright flashes from beneath those dark
Showed a heart that was gentle, a little enraged.
But quick after the storm came the sunshine so warm,
    As it burst through the clouds with a gladdening
        surprise;
I could see that her heart had forgiven the smart,
For it beamed in her beautiful, beautiful eyes.

What a look of abiding, holy faith, and confiding,
    She gave me when I told her I loved her alone,—
With her fair forehead stooping, and her eyelids all
        drooping,
    As she listened in silence I thought her my own.
Oh! the looks she then gave me are the ones that en-
        slave me,   [plies,
Though her lips gave no words I had had my re-
And they ever will chain me, haply, charm and sus-
        tain me,—
Yes, those beautiful, *beautiful*, BEAUTIFUL EYES.

"Then trilled a youthful poet's soul,—old men
    Who love, love deeply, it oft lasts for years;
When she, the subject of their tongue or pen,
    Has heavenward flown, their hot unwelcome tears
Are brushed in secret; unto Poe, how dear
Was "Lost Lenore." List to the Engineer.

Chowder.

Poe and his Annabel Lee.

When the angels had witnessed the love that existed
   On the earth, for one Annabel Lee,   [parted,
They adjudged it hard-hearted the twain should be
   It was not as they'd like it to be;
For his constancy proved that in heaven above,
They had no more undying devotional love
   Than was his by the billowy sea.

" Sure, a soul of such worth should not dwell on the
   earth,"
Said they all, "and it ought to be free;   [united,
Yes, the blooming and blighted should now be re-
   And our own should their dwelling-place be.
For the heart of poor Poe is most broken with woe,
He has no consolation in regions below,
   For the loss of his Annabel Lee."

" So, some angel must hover around this poor lover,
   In his home by the treacherous sea;
And when his heart is riven, it may guide unto heaven
   His pure spirit so faultless and free;
Where his darling and bride in her glory and pride,
His day-star shall forever be there by his side,—
   Brightly beautiful Annabel Lee."

Poe and Annabel Lee.

When October's stern blast went most drearily past
   .His lone home by the musical sea,   [ly dwelling
And the wild winds were swelling round the last earth-
    Of the beautiful Annabel Lee;   [cloud,
While the tempest was loud, a chill blast from the
Wandered wailing around the poor, noble and proud-
    Hearted Poe, and his spirit was free.

Then an angel, instructed, his spirit conducted
    From his hut by the tempest-tossed sea,
To a beautiful region, where lovers in legion
    Are as angels, and only can be;
Then they all were delighted who saw them united,
For the love that he bore her they knew was requited
    By the beautiful Annabel Lee.

Now, they hold sweet communion in spiritual union
    With the faithful, the faultless and free;   [them
For the angels around them, with glory have crowned
    With the gems from "down under the sea."
Ah! would any dissever these lovers? No, never!
But their souls shall in union dwell ever and ever,—
    Happy Poe and his Annabel Lee.

"I think I'll wake a sympathizing chord
    In most men's hearts, if I but strike my own;
Time brings no change; I recollect the word,—

Chowder.

The day, the look, the action and the tone,—
Her beauties constellated bright as Orion,
In love's young dream,"—give ear to the Historian.

The Old District School House.

Oh, how dear to us all is the fond recollection
   Of our happiest days, when we first went to school;
'T is a mournfully pleasant and long retrospection
   Of the scholars, or teacher with old beechen rule;
Of the tall spreading elm, and the stump that stood
     by it,
   Where we 've often times hid in our infantile plays,
Of the spring in the meadow, the bullrushes nigh it,
   But the most, the old school house where passed
     our young days.
Why, how suddenly ceased all our youthful commo-
     tion,   [would call,
   When from play on the green the school-mistress
And we hurried to join in her morning devotion,—
   To attend to the prayer that was given for all.
Ah! how well I remember one bright sunny morning,
   I was tempted, unthinking, to play by the way,—
How she feelingly, sweetly administered warning
   That I shall not forget until life's latest day.
For my playmate, by chance, was a neighbor's young
     daughter,—
   I was holding the dandelions under her chin;

The Old District School House.

In a moment of transport I blushingly caught her,—
  (What a terrible tumult my bosom was in),—
As she made no resistance I tremblingly kissed her,
  Made the flowers into curls to bedeck her soft hair;
She seemed nearer and dearer by far than a sister,—
  Is it strange we were late, or that scholars did stare?

Now, how oft do we dream of the sweet smiling faces,
  Of the boys and the girls whom we once used to meet;
They appear to us still to be there in their places,
  And the solemn old teacher is still in his seat.
Now, their tasks being o'er how the children are bounding
  For the closet and basket containing their meal,
And with loud shouts of gladness the air is resounding,
  Not a thought mars their future,—how happy they feel.

Now, the school-house is gone and those children have vanished,
  They are mated and scattered all over the land;
All the joy of the street now forever is banished,
  For Old Time has swept 'round with his withering hand.
But the noble old elm is in majesty growing,
  And the stump at its side still in silence decays;
As the brook from the spring in the valley is flowing,
  So my heart is the same as in infantile days.
VIII.

Chowder.

"The course of true love never did run smooth,"
So Shakspeare said, and so, of course, say I,—
(We use one straw for cider.) What can soothe
The wounded feelings? Every day I try
To laugh the matter off; grief will persist,
And "sticks like tar;" so says the Humorist.

The Ricketty Stile.

When I was very young indeed,
   I really thought of marriage,
Till one unlucky incident
   Gave all my hopes miscarriage.
I fell in love with a buxom lass,
   And sparked her quite a while;
I often think I'd have married her,
   But for an old ricketty stile.

This lass was very fond of beaux,
   Whom she was fond of jilting,
Which I knew not when I engaged
   To see her home from quilting.
We laughed, and talked, and walked along,
   I reckon about a mile,
Until we reached her father's yard,
   And that old ricketty stile.

To aid her o'er I lent my hand,
   No beau could e'er be bolder,

The Ricketty Stile.

And yet in spite of all my pains,
   She tumbled on my shoulder.
Of course I felt some slight chagrin,
   For she had smashed my tile,
And silently, but heartily,
   I blamed the ricketty stile.

I caught the maiden in my arms,
   And tried to do it gently,
While she was breathing in my face,
   And looking so intently.
Her little heart beat on my breast,
   Her lips did sweetly smile,
And so I kissed the smiles from them,
   And blessed the ricketty stile.

Now, after that for one short year,
   I used to go to see her,
And take her out to balls and rides,
   And no one could be freer.
We liked to stroll on moonlight nights,
   With hearts devoid of guile,
And every time that I returned,
   I blessed that ricketty stile.

But once upon a moonlight eve,
   When I had got belated,
She was returning from her walk,—
   I saw that she was mated.

Chowder.

And when *they* reached that ticklish spot,
  There, just as slick as *ile*,
I saw her stumble, trip, and fall
  Right over that ricketty stile.
Well, *he* was there, as I had been,
  And so, of course, he caught her,
Then he hugged her, and she hugged him,
  Exactly as I'd taught her.
While they were taking great delight,
  You may bet my blood did *bile*,
And ever since that *div'lish* day
  I've blamed the ricketty stile.

Parmenus, you're at fault; that plan is old;
  It's not the way to woo and win a woman,
The warmest spoken words will soon grow cold
  With women, old or young, and, as they're human,
They love to kiss sweet words, so write your charmer
Love sonnets, long and sweet, like me, the Farmer.

The Declaration.

Go ask yon noble river not to flow,
  Require the passing breeze to give no sigh,
Urge summer's sun to melt not winter's snow,
  Ask flowers to spring, to blossom not, and die.
Desire the lightning flashing through the oak
  To make no mark, no record of its stroke;
Ask what you will, but do not ask of me
  To still a heart that only beats for thee.

VIII.

The Declaration.

The grand Saint Lawrence with its thousand isles,
A mirror lies around each emerald child,
Reflecting frowns of heaven, as well as smiles,
No ripple roughs it by a breeze beguiled;
It glides forever onward to the sea,
In all its priceless, peerless purity,—
   So my poor heart, unmoved by love or fears,
   Hath tranquil been for many, many years.

But follow down a little in its course,
   And see its waters dashed upon the shore;
They plunge and surge with most resistless force,
   And make the wildest music in their roar.
They boil and foam among the craggy rocks,
That trembling turn the tumult of the shocks,—
   So my poor heart that long hath been so free,
   Is torn and tossed, and dashed to foam by thee.

When sweet south breezes glide among the flowers,
   And whisper stories of their journey there,
The tender leaflets, touched by magic powers,
   Will rustle, trill with every breath of air.
The finest, sweetest music heaven can give,
Is breathed in trees, and bids all nature live,—
   And thus my heart, when zephyrs only blew,
   Made music only,—music sweet and new.

But when the winds, increasing to a gale,
   The forest sweep with a tremendous power,

Chowder.

And make the feathered songsters flee and quail,
  In deepest darkness of the midnight hour,
The music ceases, and the deafening noise
Perhaps increases, and the charm destroys,—
  My heart like frightened birds' weak plaintive tones,
  Wails in my breast, or like the night wind moans.

In Alpine vales the wondrous glaciers grow,
  A vast collection from an hundred peaks,
Each sends a mighty avalanche of snow
  From cloud-capped cone, that milder region seeks,
Where warmed by sun perhaps a thousand years,
At length is moved and melted into tears,—
  So my cold heart, another Mer de Glace,
  Is warmed by smiles o'er thy dear face that pass.

All Nature glories in a wealth of flowers,
  That spring in beauty's ever endless throng,
The graceful, waving trees make shady bowers,
  A fit retreat for gay-plumed birds of song. [care,
But trees and flowers, when pruned and trimmed with
A sweeter fragrance shed, and grow more fair,—
  So would my heart, a weed or ragged tree,
  In beauty blossom, if but loved by thee.

Oft have we seen, far in the western sky,
  Two cloudlets, which the bright declining sun
Hath tinged with rainbow's richest, gorgeous dye,
  Embrace, dissolve, and mingle into one.

Mary Blake.

The spark electric, though it was unseen,
Inaudible, had surely passed between,—
   The electric flash of Love has stricken me,—
My mind, my *heart*, my SOUL's absorbed in THEE.

Come, Sam, do give us something nice and new,
   Fresh as a field where forests lately stood;
Where odorous coal-pits burn, where sun and dew
   Revivify the soil; where mouldering wood
Is thrown in heaps; where corn is lately planted,
And you can smell the earth, that's what is wanted.

Mary Blake.

In yonder rustic cottage hard by the silver lake,
There lives my little darling—I call her Mary Blake.
I know I love her truly, and she has loved me long;
Oh, when I serenade her, then this shall be my song.

Chorus.—Come love, come, my boat is by the shore,
The breeze will fill the snowy sail, I will hold the oar;
   Come, love, come, and gaily let us roam,
I'll take thee o'er the waters to my mountain home.

The stars are shining brightly from homes up in the skies,
But do not beam as brilliant as my true lover's eyes;
The apple trees in spring time with fragrance load the air, [fair.
But have not that deliciousness floating round my

VIII.   *Chorus.*

Chowder.

The moon is smiling sweetly on valley and on lake,
But does not smile so sweetly as winning Mary Blake;
The birds that carol lightly to partners in the grove,
Have voices without melody compared with her's I love. *Chorus.*

Don't boast to me of beauties of Scotland, Spain or France, [dance.
She reigns the belle of Newcomb at every country
If waving grain is graceful no longer would you prate,
But vote her queen of motion if you could see her skate. *Chorus.*

Your girls can play pianos, can draw, perhaps, and paint, [would faint.
Mine makes her music spinning when city belles
They ride in costly carriage, in omnibus or hack,
My own her courser catches and mounts upon his back. *Chorus.*

You long to own a mansion that's nestled by the sea,
But give to me my cottage with scenery wild and free;
The wooded hills around me,—a maiden true and coy,
Where thought can roam unfettered, and hearts leap up for joy. *Chorus.*

Come, Nick, now give us one step farther back,
  Where love's unswayed by etiquette or art,
Where men and women follow nature's track,

O-ra-la Loo.

No wealth allures, position forms no part,
But like seeks like, unyielding as the fates,
Where love wins love, as songsters choose their mates.

O-ra-la Loo.

'T is some five years ago I first happened to find
A most beautiful maiden who suited my mind.
I was guiding a party on big Tupper's Lake,
And by chance overtook her and rowed in her wake.
Her old father was trolling and handled the line,
   Not a ripple was seen on the water's bright blue,
Saving only the tremble that followed the twine,
   For so lightly she paddled the birch-bark canoe.

It so happened our camp-fires were lighted that night
Near a spring whose cool waters were limpid and bright;
We were seeking its nook for some water for tea,
And our paths came together—an omen for me.
There together we dipped from the well shaded pool,
   As we filled our small vessels, not saying a word;
We arose, our eyes met; oh, I felt like a fool,
   Like one frightened, she fluttered and flew like a [bird.

In the moonlight I strolled by the beach of the lake,
With a mind, as you know, such a meeting would make,
And we met by a sharp point of rocks near the bay;
In the Indian tongue I implored her to stay.

Chowder.

"Oh coy maiden," I said, "tell me whom do you seek?
    Can it be for a lover who 'll ever prove true?"
As her eyelashes fell she endeavored to speak,
    But I understood only "I'm looking for you."

There we sat on a rock where the bright ripples rolled,
And the buds of our love did in blossoms unfold;
I related my life truly, frankly, and she
Gave her own with an answering freedom to me.
Then I offered my hand, asking hers in return,
    Making promises wild, such as all lovers do;
"Ah! your promise is air, all your offers I spurn,
    Till you overtake me in my birch-bark canoe."

How I flew for my boat, pushed it off from the shore,
Quickly leaped to the seat and adjusted each oar,
Rowed around by the point that just sheltered the bay,
Where the challenging maid in her fairy boat lay.
As she started, the paddle she skillfully plied,
    And put out for an island but faintly in view,
How I struggled half frantic with love, hope and pride,
    In the wake of the girl in the birch-bark canoe.

As we came near the island she slackened her pace,
And a smile of compassion came over her face;
Though I pulled like a buck, she could flee like a doe,
It was useless, my trying to catch her, I know.
Side by side on the beach our two little boats lay
    Till the moon could no longer gild diamonds of
            dew;   VIII.

The Young Folks from Home.

We returned to the camp by the spring in the bay,
But no St. Regis maid in the birch-bark canoe.

"Come, Cæsar, you must finish this programme."
" Excuse me, sir, I have n't washed the dishes,
Because I stopped and listened, sir, to Sam
 And other gents, and I must dress these fishes,
And have all things prepared for breakfast early,
Or, otherwise, 'twill all be hurly-burly.

Let 's have another round, it 's early yet,
 And let the themes be varied as your lives,
Save, if you owe to sadness any debt,
 Pay that to-morrow ; merriment but thrives
On recollections of our happiest hours,—
Now, please, Professor, exercise your powers.

The Young Folks from Home.

Oh! who does not remember that season of joy,
In the spring time of life which no age can destroy ;
When our heart-beats were light and our minds un-
 restrained   [chained ;
As the breeze o'er the mountains, or leopards un-
When regrets for the past were so sweetly destroyed,
And the present alone was the moment enjoyed ;
When no thought of the future unwelcome could come
To intrude on the pleasures of young folks from home.

VIII.

Chowder.

When occasion convened us, how happy were all,
At the party or pic-nic, or wedding, or ball.
Oh! how swiftly, how sweetly the time flew along,
As we reveled in dances or joined in the song.
On the billows of fancy we gaily were tossed,
And the moments of care were the moments we lost,
For the mind, like the needle, will oftentimes roam,
And yet seek for its Pole Star, the young folks from home.

The old miser finds pleasure in counting his gold,
And the young antiquary in things that are old.
The fond beau in the beam of his mistress's eyes,
The astronomer nightly in viewing the skies;
But we may have a pleasure far dearer than those,
We may feel all their ecstacy,—none of their woes;
It is dearer by far than the musty old tome [home.
To the poet, when meeting with young folks from

Fare ye well, happy time! though you never return,
Still, thy praises we'll sing, for our bosoms yet burn
With the thought of the past, when so freely we roved
In those groves of enchantment and fancy we loved.
Oh! our breast's like the ocean, when placid and deep
In which memory seems to be sweetly asleep.
Till the heart, like the tempest that dashes the foam,
Leaps aloft, when we think of the young folks from home. VIII.

My Native Hills.

Come now, you Wanderer of the beauteous earth,
  And chant the praises of the dearest scene
Your path has crossed, if it awoke to birth
  A stave, a thought, or feeling; did you glean
Some gorgeous shell you hold in memory dear,
That will the tale repeat to listening ear?

My Native Hills.

I 've often gazed with love and pride
  Upon that graceful range,
As looks the bridegroom on his bride
  And thinks she 'll never change.
Though absent far, in memory yet
  My heart instinctive thrills,
For those loved spots, I ne'er forget—
  My own, my native hills.

The traveler in a foreign clime
  Where Art shines so supreme,
And Nature seems much more sublime,
  Where countless beauties teem,
Still finds a theme in home-made joy;
  His bursting bosom fills
With recollections of the boy
  Upon his native hills.

The artist, who, with skillful hand,
  And colors rich and rare,
Depicts bright scenes in native land

Chowder.

    Upon his canvass fair,
The poet, too, with pen of truth,
    In every heart instills
A love of home, where, as a youth,
    He roamed his native hills.

Lives there a man who 's highland born,
    Though he be gray and old,
Who treats his hailing-place with scorn?
    Whose heart has grown so cold?
No! when he tells of happy hours,
    Though life has seemed all ills,
A gleam of sunshine through life's showers,
    Illumes his native hills.

Now, gentle Poet, let your dulcet strain
  Ring through the forest like a whippowill,
Till song-birds, wakened, join in the refrain,
  And rouse the echoes which have long been still,
Let murmuring rivers aid you, woods profound
Shall trill in gladness at the welcome sound.

    O-ri-o-la Loo-Lee.

Golden-breasted oriole, sable-crested oriole,
  When you 've rested, oriole, on my maple tree,
Will you sing a song for me, one that 's merry, wild
    and free,
  Filled with gladness rich with glee? Oriolalee,
If I 'll give my thanks to thee? O-ri-o-la Loo-lee.

VIII.

O-ri-o-la Loo-lee.

You with plumage strange and bright, borne with pinions dark as night,
And a heart that seems so light, on my maple tree,
Sing for me your sweetest song, gaily, gushing, full and strong,
Warble clearly, loud and and long, Oriolalee,
Dearest of the singing throng, O-ri-o-la Loo-lee.

Now I hear the joyous note issuing from your tiny throat,
On the air it seems to float, like foam upon the sea;
Sing away, you need not fear, nothing now will harm you here,
Let it echo loud and clear, Oriolalee,
Till all birds shall stop to hear, O-ri-o-la Loo-lee.

" From a southern land we've come, long and weary did we roam,
Till we found a happy home, in your maple tree,
On this bough I've often sung, on that branch our nest is hung,
In the nest my mate is swung, Oriolalee,
Rearing patiently our young, O-ri-o-la Loo-lee.

When comes round the autumn time we shall seek a warmer clime, [tree,
There again I'll sing my rhyme on some orange
There again my mate shall swing, with our brood which we will bring,
All the day the grove shall ring, Oriolalee,
Living in perpetual spring, O-ri-o-la Loo-lee."

Chowder.

Happy little bird of fire, could I have my heart's desire,
    I, likewise, would never tire, singing from a tree;
Life in peace should glide along, void of strife and
    free from wrong,
Night and morning, all day long, Oriolalee,
Singing an unending song, O-ri-o-la Loo-lee.

Come, Engineer, and build for us a song,
    Lay out your line of thought with skill and science,
Make your location right, or else all wrong
    Will be the end thereof; none in defiance
Of certain rules can labor. Crockett said,
" Be sure you 're right, my friend, then go ahead."

The Song of the Engineer.

Though a wandering life a poor Engineer leads,
    His lone pathway is ever delicious and bright,
For in anticipation he rarely exceeds
    What reality brings him of joy and delight;
Though his sorrows are few, and his cares quickly fade,
    He most freely adopts the philosopher's plan;
Taking men as they are, and the world as 'twas made,
    Acting nobly his part in life's drama—a man.

See, the line of his life is as true to the mark,
    As the transit of conscience that acts as his guide;
For his back-sight's a check, when his foresight looks
    dark,

The Song of the Engineer.

He thus rights all his errors, for right is his pride.
　The long picket before is the beacon of hope,
　The short picket behind is experience's flame,
While the range of his glass, like his intellect's scope,
　Gives his course and his bearing from honor or fame.

Though his life be a series of up and down grades,
　He can truly and faithfully level them all;
When the prospects look dull, all the murkiness fades
　If he sums up his rise, disregarding his fall;
Though his spirits may flutter like those in his glass,
　They most surely will seek in their level to stay,
Yielding calmly, resigned to the shadows that pass,
　And exult in their pride when the clouds clear away.

His pure heart is his target, its index his face,
　And the cross-lines ambition and excellence are;
To the lady he loves it will bring no disgrace,
　'Tis as true as the needle that points to the star.
Sure, the chain of his life is exact as the chain
　That he carries, its links of affection as pure
As its steel, and it safely will bear any strain,
　It will never corrode while his life shall endure.

In his youth he constructs a substantial foundation,
　One on which a most beautiful structure to rear,—
For his base truth and virtue, each course, education,
　Is cemented by patience and practice; each pier

Chowder.

Is supporting the arch; there are justice and honor,
   Faith, hope, love and charity, friendship combined
With peace, temperance, fortitude, purity, candor,
   Firmly held by the key, independence of mind.

Will the Historian please to condescend,
   And give to us a diamond in the rough,—
Some simple thing that we can comprehend,
   No mythologic tale, nor legend tough;
But something tender, touching, terse and tart,
That every man can feel who's got a heart.

The Chains of Memory.

There is a chain more dear than gold, that binds me
    to the past,   [hold me fast.
And though the links are worn and old, they still can
How lightly did I value them when they were newly
    formed,   [heart has warmed.
But now they're each a treasured gem that oft my

This little chain of memories bright, of hope, and
    love, and joy,   [alloy,
That fills my soul with fond delight, without the least
I would not break, though half the earth were offered
    in its place,   [not efface.
For fancy thoughts ne'er had a birth that time did

But there's a chain more strong than steel, that I
    would break with joy,   VIII.

Excuses.

Each day its heavy folds I feel, and yet cannot destroy;
The links are grief and hope deferred, with mournful
   memories twined,   [be defined.
And vain regrets when prudence erred, that cannot

Ah! who has not this double chain, these links of
   good and ill,   [mortal skill;
That mingle pleasure in with pain with more than
Those who have not, if such there are, enjoy a heaven
   here,   [dropped the tear.
But greatest of the number far, are those who've

Already, Smartweed? surely you can sing,
"The bird that can and won't," you know the rest;
Well, if you're not a bird, you are a thing
   They call a goose. You'll not forsake your nest?
Suppose they do get cold? of course they're addle,
Well squawk or sing, if here, or else skedaddle.

Excuses.

Dear friends! why will you urge me thus?
   You know, you know I cannot sing,
Your presence seems an incubus,
   A strange and most uncommon thing.
I used to carol like a bird,
   When breathed I free my native air,
But now my voice can scarce be heard,
   My heart is sinking in despair,
Because I cannot sing to-night, to-night.

Chowder.

I 'm so embarrassed by a crowd,
    My voice attempts to flee from me,
It once was mellow, high and loud,
    But now so weak as scarce to be
Above the whispering of the breeze;
    My heart so beats within my breast,
It seems as though my blood would freeze,
    Whene'er I try to do my best.
But do n't you see I cannot, cannot sing.

There are so many near me now,
    Who 've often been to singing schools,
And learned from books and teachers how
    To read the notes and sing by rules,
Who are so skilled in flats and sharps,
    Scales, pitches, keys, time, tune and tone,
I wake no echo in their harps,
    And have to chant my stave alone.
Oh! can't you see I cannot sing to-night.

My songs have grown so stale and old,
    I 'm sure you cannot wish to hear;
When I have such a horrid cold
    Much more defective they appear;
I have an awful headache, too,
    The room, of course is much too tight,
I pray that you 'll excuse me, do!
    Because I cannot sing to-night,
I cannot sing, I cannot sing to-night.

Boys in Blue.

I've called on all the heathen gods,
  To lend me succor in my song,
But invocation makes no odds,
  There must of course be something wrong;
The ruling god of poetry,
  At each and every effort weeps
The tuneful muse of harmony,
  Her angry face averted keeps,
Because I cannot, cannot sing to-night.

Come, Samuel, you of course will lend an oar,
  *(*I'd like myself to close this concertation*),*
Sing something patriotic; you've a score
  Of noble songs; sing praises of the nation,—
We can't excuse you; if you've nothing new,
Take something old then, take the "Boys in Blue."

Boys in Blue.

When the red cloud of war overshadowed our land,
  And the people, awakened, stood trembling with fear;
When the demon Secession, with dagger in hand,
  Stood demanding the jewel each freeman holds dear;
When the clarion voice of our Chief called "to arms,"
  And proclaimed that the Nation must strive for its life; [farms,
Who were they that deserted their workshops and

Chowder.

And then seizing the musket rushed into the strife?
'T was the Boys in Blue, yes, the Boys in Blue,
With their eyes on the foe and with hearts ever true;
Oh, none nobler, none braver the world ever knew,
Than the patriot souls of these Boys in Blue.

When disgrace and disaster o'erwhemingly fell
   On our arms in a nobly and fairly fought field;
When the news of defeat struck our hearts like a knell,
   And the cowards and traitors implored us to yield;
When the cowardly chief of the seven days' strife,
   Though victorious, trailed our proud flag in the dust;
Who were they that the Nation then looked to for life,
   And in whom did the people implicitly trust?
     'T was the Boys in Blue, yes, &c.

When gaunt famine and death stared them full in the face,
   In the prisons surrounded by insolent foes;
When at Libby, Belle Isle, or that blot of disgrace,
   Horrid Andersonville, where our heroes repose;
When a lingering starvation was surely their fate,
   If our army or peace did not bring them release;
Who were they that cried "Fight, we can suffer and wait,   [peace?"
When the rebels are conquered, then think of a
     'T was the Boys in Blue, yes, &c.

Nature's Music.

When the conflict was ended and Peace once again
    Spread her sorrowful wings o'er our desolate land;
When the thinned ranks of labor were filling with men,
    And our officers ceased to give words of command;
When old monarchs were anxiously waiting to hear
    Of disorder they said that was surely to be;
Who were they that taught them whom they'd reason to fear,   [FREE?
That this Nation, self-governed, was mighty and
    'T was the Boys in Blue, yes, &c.

Now, Nick, your turn is next; my forest child
    Sure will not fail me at a time like this,
Give melody the rein, let "wood-notes wild"
    Ring through the alleys of this dark abyss,
This tangled forest in secluded vale,
A joyous strain and not a mourner's wail.

Nature's Music.

Untutored by teachers, untrammeled by rules,
    Our wild notes in freedom we sing,
Unguided by masters, ungoverned by schools,
    And fresh from our bosoms they spring.
Ha! the wild woodland notes
That come forth from our throats,
    As we carol in innocent glee,
Are promptings of nature
In language and feature,
    And that is the music for me.
VIII.

Chowder.

The murmuring rill, as it glides down the hill,
    Wakes music in moving along,
The birds on the trees can delight if they please,
    And happily join in the song.
Ha! their notes are as wild
As the laugh of a child,
    When singing in innocent glee;
This music of nature
Delights ev'ry creature,
    And this is the music for me.

The tempest's wild roar on a rocky bound shore,
    Is music both boundless and deep,
The maddened waves roll, never knowing control,
    So changeful no form can they keep.
Ha! the quick beating shocks,
As they strike on the rocks,
    Give music sublime, wild and free,
'T is the music of nature
In roughest of feature,
    And this is the music for me.

When I meet with a man who no music can scan,
    My heart from the monster recoils,
The bard made a hit when he said such were " fit
    For stratagem, treason and spoils."
Ha! they are of no worth,
They 're the pest of the earth,

Old John Brown.

From them all we should ever be free,
Then musical nature
In every creature,
Would make sweetest music for me.

Now, Cæsar, let your rich, melodious strain
  Ring as it used to in the southern land,
When serried ranks swept o'er the slippery plain,
  With flashing bayonet and glittering brand.
Recount to us the glory and renown
That wreathes the famous name of Old John Brown.

Old John Brown.

Old John Brown had a very little army,
Old John Brown had a slightly little army,
Old John Brown had a mighty little army
  Of just about twenty men.
He marched away down South as far as old Virginny,
Where a big buck nigger sells for as much as fifty guinea, [ninny,
With a corresponding price for his wife and picca-
  To pick the cotton on a Georgia plantation.
He captured Harper's Ferry in about a half a minute,
'T was a very pretty village with five thousand people in it, [spin it,
There's a long yarn about it, but I have n't time to
  Betwixt now and next November.

Chowder.

Old John Brown had a very little army,
Old John Brown, " Old Ossawattamie,"
Old John Brown of Essex County,
   Away up in the Adirondacks.
But chivalrous Virginia, who is there to upbraid her,
She rallied forty thousand men to stop the bold invader,   [her,
With gallant little Maryland and Uncle Sam to aid
   Surrounded and captured an empty school house ;
If Old Brown's army had been a little bigger,
About two white men and one little nigger,
He 'd have conquered old Virginny and would never pulled a trigger,
   On the fruitful banks of the old Potomac.

Old John Brown had a very little army,
Old John Brown had a dashing little army,
Old John Brown's heroic little army
   Of just about twenty men.   [slavery haters,
To hunt with hounds these twenty men, consistent
To brand their names with infamy, and hang them
   up like traitors,   [pertaters,"
If this is "southern chivalry," 't is very "small
   Too few in the hill to pay for digging.
Twenty, eighteen, sixteen, fourteen,
Twelve, ten, eight, six, four, two, none,
Nineteen, seventeen, fifteen, thirteen,
   Eleven, nine, seven, five, three and one.

Old John Brown.

Old John Brown had a very little army,
Old John Brown had a gallant little army,
Old John Brown had a daring little army
    Of just about twenty men. [prison,
Old Henry Wise, he caught him and put him in a
If Brown had been in Wise's place, and Wise had
    been in *his 'n*, [risen,
Do you think that such an army ever would have
    Way down in the Old Dominion? [elected,
As there surely would have been had Fremont been
As many men strove nobly for, and honestly expected;
If Wise had seized the arsenal, would he have been
    ejected
    By the "F. F. V.'s" and J. B.'s minions?

For comfort or counsel they gave him no season,
But put him on trial on charges of treason,
Proved him guilty, of course, without right or reason,
    That would bring a blush on the face of nature.
As he marched to his doom with his neck in the halter,
His step was still firm, and his voice did not falter,
A martyr to freedom on liberty's altar,—
    Old John Brown!
'Mid the names of the heroes that we shall hand down
Unto all future ages as worthy a crown,
High, high! on the list is the name of John Brown,—
    Old John Brown.

Chowder.

And for each of the twenty who sank to his grave,
A million will rise just as bold and as brave,
Till this " land of the free " holds no longer a slave,
 Old John Brown.

Good Night.

What joys untold the mother feels,
 What hopes, what pleasure rare,
When by her side her infant kneels,
 To lisp its evening prayer.
How piously those tones ascend,
 Unconscious of their might;
What consolation seems to blend
 With those sweet words, " Good night."
_{" Good night, mama."} " Good night, my child."
_{" Good night, papa."} " Good night."

Oh! who can paint the maiden's grief,
 When lovers bid adieu?
What balm can give her soul relief?
 What joy her hopes renew?
How beats her heart with hopes and fears,
 Each striving for the might,
With voice suppressed and eyes in tears,
 She hears the sad " Good night."
" Good night, my love." " Good night, my dear."
" My light," " my life, good night."

But different feelings fill the soul
　Of him who sings to you;
O'er joy and grief he's no control,
　Or visions bright and new.
His griefs no maiden ever knew,
　No mother his delight,
A grateful heart that's beating true,
　Prompts him to say "Good night."
"Good night, my friends; good night, old woods;
Good night, ye stars, good night."

As we proposed, we broke up camp next day,
　And in the course of time we reached Crown Point,
Somewhat fatigued with riding that rough way,
　With bodies bruised and limbs near out of joint.
We parted then and there, our last adieu
Was just as silent as is mine to you.
　VIII. 990

RECAPITULATION.

Professor, - - - - -	792
Traveler, - - - - - -	963
Poet, - - - - - -	960
Engineer, - - - - -	1,028
Historian, - - - - -	1,018
Humorist, - - - - - -	1,012
Farmer, - - - - - -	1,014
Chowder, - - - - - -	990
Total lines, - - - -	7,777

www.ingramcontent.com/pod-product-compliance
Lightning Source LLC
Chambersburg PA
CBHW030311240426
43673CB00040B/1125